How Your Body Works

Other Science Books by the Same Authors

Let's Find Out

About Heat, Water, and Air—with Experiments

Now Try This

Friction, Levers, Inclined Planes, and Wheels—with Experiments

Let's Look Inside Your House

Your Home's Water, Heat, and Electricity—with Experiments

How Big Is Big?

A Yardstick for the Universe from Stars to Atoms

HOW
Your Body Works

By Herman Schneider
Science Coordinator, New York City Public Schools
and Nina Schneider

Introduction by MILTON I. LEVINE, M.D.
Assistant Professor of Pediatrics, Cornell University
New York Hospital Medical Center, New York

With Illustrations by BARBARA IVINS

WILLIAM R. SCOTT, INC., PUBLISHER
NEW YORK

First Printing October, 1949
Second Printing April, 1950
Third Printing November, 1952
Fourth Printing June, 1954
Fifth Printing September, 1956
Sixth Printing May, 1958
Seventh Printing December, 1959
Eighth Printing November, 1960
Ninth Printing December, 1962

Table Of Contents

You Own A Wonderful Machine

The world is full of many wonderful and extremely complicated machines—machines that our grandparents never even heard of. There are airplanes so constructed that the pilot can tell at a glance how high he is, how fast he is traveling, and whether he is traveling in the right direction. There are wonderful machines like radio and television. There are machines that add, subtract, multiply, and divide.

But no machine is as wonderful as your own body. Just think about it a little.

No machine can see and hear and smell and taste and feel. No machine can laugh or cry or get angry. And no machine can grow.

But all living things grow at some time in their lives —kittens grow into cats, puppies into dogs, tadpoles into frogs, and little yellow baby chicks into hens and roosters. All of us have had fun taking care of animals and watching them grow. Do you remember what you fed them and how fast they grew?

Have you ever watched a baby grow? Most babies weigh six or seven pounds when they are born. They have very little hair, if any, and no teeth. They are unable to sit up or even to roll over. Their food is nothing but milk for the first few months, and then gradually they begin to eat cereal, fruits, and vegetables.

In five months a baby weighs about 14 pounds—he has doubled his weight at birth. When he is one year old the baby weighs about 21 pounds—three times as much as he weighed the day he was born. Imagine if next year you weighed three times as much as you weigh now!

Other exciting things are also happening as the baby grows. More hair appears on his head, and little white teeth cut through the gums. His muscles grow firmer and stronger. When he is about six months old the baby is able to sit up by himself, and when he is about a year old he is usually able to take his first step.

Some of the milk that the baby drank went to form skin, some went to form muscle, some formed blood, some formed bone, some formed hair, and some formed teeth. It sounds like magic. Did you ever wonder how it happened?

Here is an interesting book which will help you answer this and many more questions about your body. I'm sure you will enjoy it.

MILTON I. LEVINE, M.D.

PART ONE
How Your Body Uses Food

1. Food — From Taste To Digestion

Everywhere, all over the world, right at this minute, children are eating green peas, chopped blubber, raw fish, shashlik, rice, pemmican, roast beef. They eat so that they can grow and be strong.

All over the world people eat, but no matter what kind of food they eat, people look like people. Their heads are not heads of lettuce, their legs are not legs of lamb, their eyes are not eyes of potatoes, and their ears don't look like ears of corn.

Every person, no matter what kind of foods he eats, has a head, a body, arms and legs. Everyone is wrapped in skin—waterproof, snug, and of exactly the right size and shape. Under the skin, everybody has big muscles that can lift heavy things and delicate muscles that can hold a pencil and dot an "i," and hundreds of other muscles of all shapes and sizes to make him bend, turn, run, stand, and move in all the ways people move.

Whether the favorite family dish is squirrel stew or sirloin steak, every person—man, woman, or child—has 206 bones that are shaped to protect his insides and support the body either at rest or in motion.

All of us have a brain and a stomach and a heart fixed in their places, and blood that moves in and out of all those places all over our body. No matter where we come from or where we go, we can grow, can feel, and can think.

We all grow and get strong from the food we eat. No one has ever invented another way. Eskimo or African, we all need food. But how does the food you eat turn into the things your body needs to help you grow and be strong?

Eating Is Just The Beginning

Many different things happen to food before it becomes part of you. When you look at the turkey bones on your plate and say, "I can't eat another bite. I'm *finished* with dinner!" you've really just begun. Only part of the job is finished, the part of getting the food *in*. Now the food must be worked on until it becomes just what the different parts of your body need for growing, for work, and for play. Your body doesn't have to learn what to do. It knows its job and every part sets to work changing food into you. The job takes several hours or more. The first part of the job is called DIGESTION.

Tasting

Digestion begins when you taste food. You know that you taste with your tongue. But do you know what other part you use in tasting? This part is even more important than your tongue. Here is a way to find out what that part is.

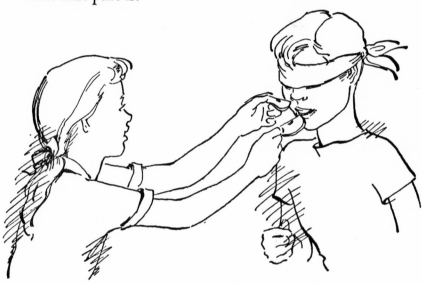

TASTE EXPERIMENT

YOU WILL NEED: a slice of apple cut into thin pieces, a small slice of pear cut into thin pieces, and a friend any size, but not in pieces.

TRY THIS. Tell your friend to shut his eyes. Hold the piece of pear under his nose and put a piece of apple in his mouth. Ask him what he's eating.

You will find that he'll tell you it's a pear.

This shows that we use both nose and tongue to taste food. In fact, most of the tasting you do is with your nose. Do you know, now, why foods don't taste like much when you have a cold in the nose and can't smell?

From Mouth To Stomach

After your mouth and nose have told you that there is food, they tell you it is good to eat. If the food smells good, your mouth begins to water. You know how your mouth waters when you walk past a bakery and smell the delicious smells. The next time you sit down to a meal, take a good strong sniff of the food and feel the water coming into your mouth. The water is called saliva. Saliva wets and softens your food at the same time as your teeth chop and grind it into smaller pieces.

As the food is chopped and moistened, the tongue pushes it from side to side. When the food is ready for swallowing, the tongue pushes it back to the back of your mouth where a long tube leads the foods down to the stomach. It is a special kind of tube, because it can push the food along, instead of just letting it fall down. Here's a way to show that the food is actually *pushed* down to the stomach.

14

You will need: a small piece of candy, a glass of water or soda pop, and that friend, any size.

Try this. Help your friend to stand upside down on his head. Feed him the candy. What happens?

You will find that he will be able to chew and swallow it, even though he is upside down.

Now try this. Get your friend to stand on his head again and give him half a glass of water or soda to drink. What happens?

You will find that your friend can eat or drink upside down, but that he will tell you that it's more comfortable the usual way.

This shows that the food tube pushes the food down into your stomach. Otherwise, food would stick in the tube.

The pushing is done by little muscles in the lining of the food tube. Mouthful after mouthful, the chopped, moistened food goes down the food tube. It goes into your stomach, which can stretch to hold an entire Thanksgiving dinner, from fruit cup to pumpkin pie.

In The Stomach

Now your dinner plate is empty and your stomach is full. You feel comfortable and pleasant. Sometimes you're even a bit sleepy. You are finished eating, but your body is just beginning to change the food into the things it needs. It still has lots of inside work to do.

How does a dinner in the stomach change so that people can use it for growing and for strength? How can it be gotten ready for your growing body to turn into teeth, muscles, and bone?

First, the chunks of food have to be changed into soft, watery pulp. Your teeth began this job by chopping and grinding the food. The saliva moistened it. Now the stomach goes to work with more juices.

The stomach is a strong bag that can stretch to hold even a very big dinner. The walls of the stomach are lined with muscles. These strong muscles of the stomach churn and roll the

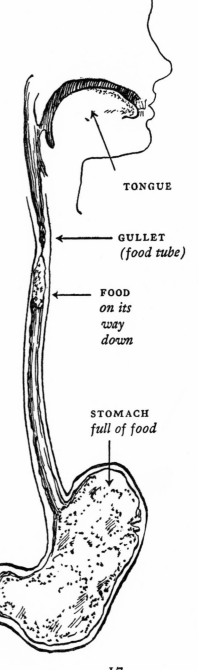

TONGUE

GULLET
(food tube)

FOOD
on its
way
down

STOMACH
full of food

INTESTINE begins here

food that was crushed by your teeth. Let's see what crushing and churning and rolling does to food.

CRUSHING EXPERIMENT

YOU WILL NEED: two lumps of sugar and two glasses of water.

TRY THIS. Put two lumps of sugar, one crushed and one whole, each in a separate glass of water. Stir each and see which one dissolves and becomes liquid more quickly.

YOU WILL FIND that the crushed lump dissolves and becomes liquid much more quickly.

THIS SHOWS that it is easier to make food into a liquid after it has been crushed into small pieces.

When your teeth chop and crush the food, the stomach is able to do its part more easily. If you swallow

18

your food without chewing it into small pieces, it is harder work for the stomach, which sometimes says so by giving you a stomach ache.

There are special juices inside the stomach. These juices make the chopped food softer and more watery. But there is something else happening to the food in the stomach to help it dissolve. It is being swished around, too. Here is an experiment to show what swishing does to food.

CHURNING EXPERIMENT

You will need: two small jars with covers, two red cinnamon drops or two small pieces of hard, colored candy.

Try this. Fill the jars with equal amounts of water. Drop a piece of candy in each jar. Cover both jars. Let one stand still. Rock the other steadily. See

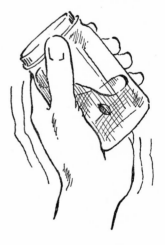

how long it takes each piece of candy to become liquid and dissolve.

YOU WILL FIND that the candy that was moved around dissolved more quickly. Swishing food around in a liquid dissolves it faster.

Of course, the liquids in your mouth and stomach aren't just water. They are many different kinds of juices and they are able to dissolve and change many different foods that won't dissolve easily in plain water.

By now, many things have happened to the food. Your teeth have chopped it, saliva has wet it and softened it, your stomach has churned it and poured juices on it. But most of it isn't quite ready yet to be used by your body. Still more work has to be done.

In The Intestine

The stomach pushes the food, a little at a time, into a long coiled tube under your stomach called the INTESTINE. This tube is four or five times as long as you are, which is why it has to be coiled to fit in the space under your stomach. Like the food tube to the stomach, this one has muscles, too, that mash the food and push it along while more juices pour on it. By the time your dinner has traveled most of the way through this tube, the food has changed a great deal. Turkey and pie have been mashed and swished and softened and dissolved until they are a liquid ready for the body.

But some of the food you eat is of no use to the body. It just doesn't have what the body needs, or the body can't make it into useful material. It is called waste, and is thrown away by the body just as you throw something that you can't use into a wastebasket.

We'll find out more about waste later on. But right now, let's see what happens to the liquid digested food which your body is going to use.

21

INTESTINE
(*coiled tube*)

2. How Food Gets Where It Is Needed

What's the use of food that just keeps moving along inside a tube? Every part of your body is waiting for it. But what good is it if it's inside a tube? The question is, how does the food get *out* of the tube to feed you?

It isn't such a simple question. The liquid food that is ready to be used has to be carried to the rest of your body. At the same time your intestine has to hold back the food that is not quite ready. There are really two big jobs here. How can the intestine do both jobs at the same time? Here is an experiment you can do that will give you an idea of how two such jobs can be done at the same time.

FILTERING EXPERIMENT

YOU WILL NEED: salt, cocoa, a paper towel, a small drinking glass, and a large drinking glass half full of water.

TRY THIS. Cut a piece of paper towel about four inches long and four inches wide. Fold it so that it forms a funnel with no hole in the bottom. Place it, with the point down, in a small glass.

Now pour a teaspoon of salt into the large glass of

water and stir it until the salt is completely dissolved. Then pour a teaspoon of cocoa into the same glass and stir until the mixture is brown. Then, *slowly*, pour the brown mixture of cocoa and salt into the paper in the little glass. Taste the water that comes through. What does it taste like?

You will find that it will taste very salty, but there will be almost no taste of cocoa. You could tell that the salt came right through the paper, because you could taste it in the water that soaked through. But most of the cocoa was held back. You could tell that because there was almost no cocoa taste and no cocoa color in the water that soaked through.

This shows how some materials can pass easily through paper, while others are held back.

The same sort of thing happens in your intestine. Food that is ready for the body can easily pass through the walls of the intestine, while the rest of the food is held back until it is completely ready, or until it is pushed out as waste.

In your intestine there are special parts, called VILLI, whose job it is to separate the ready food from the not-ready food. These parts are really much tinier than the picture shows. The ready food soaks through them, the way the salt soaked through the paper in the salt and cocoa experiment.

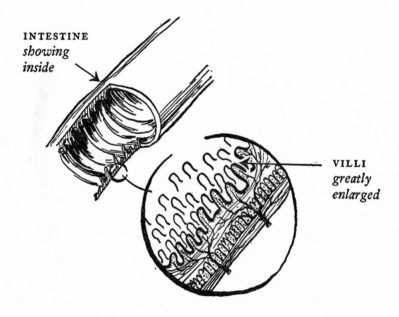

INTESTINE
showing
inside

VILLI
greatly
enlarged

Out Of The Intestine

Now that the food has soaked through the walls of the intestine, where does it go? If you're dancing or swimming, or playing the piano, you need food brought to all parts of your body that need food. If you're playing ball, you need food brought to the arm for pitching, to the legs for running bases, or to the skin to repair a scrape on the knee, perhaps. But it's a long way from your intestine to your feet or your eyes. How does the food get around?

STOMACH

INTESTINE

BLOOD
TUBES

Into Your Blood

Your body has a food transportation system. The blood is like a freight train that carries the goods. In the walls of the intestine are tiny thin tubes through which the blood moves. The liquid food soaks through the walls of the intestine, into these tiny thin tubes which are filled with blood. The blood, with the food in it, keeps moving right along. The tiny thin tubes join together to form larger tubes which lead the blood to every part of your body.

Every part of your body has blood flowing through it or very near it. You can see some of the blood tubes as bluish lines at your wrists or on the back of your hands. In other places such as your eyelids, eyeballs, and your ears, you can see pink or red lines. There are different kinds of blood tubes in your body. Some are as thin as a hair, others are as thick as your finger, but they carry the blood, with its freight, to every part of you.

When the blood flows past a part of your body where food is needed, that part gets the food it needs from the blood, through the walls of the tubes. The bones take what they need to use, the muscles take what they need, the skin takes its share; every part of the body gets its food from the blood as it flows past.

Storehouses For Extra Food

After every part of your body has been fed, there is often some good food left over, which you don't need at the moment. To store up this extra food your body has a big storehouse and lots of little storehouses. Blood carries the extra food to the big storehouse, which is called the LIVER, or to the little storehouses, which are

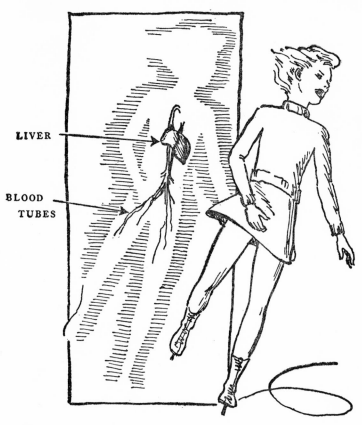

LIVER

BLOOD
TUBES

the layers of fat under your skin. Layers of fat are found almost all over the body. Fat people have thicker layers of fat than thin people, but all people have some fat stored under the skin.

When any part of the body needs food for hard, fast work, what happens? Blood flows through the liver and through the fat layers. Blood picks up the stored food and swiftly carries it to wherever it is needed.

Anywhere in the body, a call for food is answered by the blood. If you are rowing, skating, or writing, the blood rushes wherever you need it—to your hands, your arms, your brain, your feet, your back. Food is delivered all through your body by your blood.

What Keeps The Blood Moving?

But how does the blood flow steadily all through your body? You can see how it might fall down to your toes. But how does it come up to your head or into your pitching arm? What keeps the blood moving steadily, all the time, every second of the night and day all our whole lives? What keeps it moving whether we stand on our heads or on our feet, or swim, or lie down, or sleep quietly?

Your heart is the answer. Your heart is a pumping

machine about the size of your fist, with four pumps working all the time. Two of the pumps push blood out to all parts of the body, and two others suck blood back to the heart. A drop of blood takes less than a minute to make a round trip through your body.

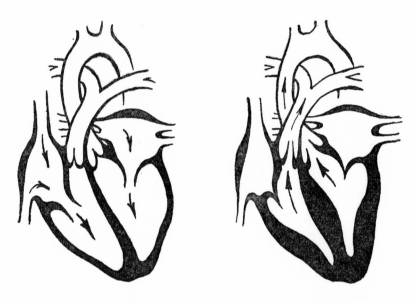

HEART PUMPING BLOOD IN AND OUT

Left: two upper pumps expand and suck blood into the heart.
Right: two lower pumps contract and pump blood out of the heart.

This is what happens during a round trip. The blood is pushed out of the heart into strong, muscular tubes called ARTERIES. These tubes go to all parts of your body. But they are too thick to reach into *every* tiny part of you, so they branch into thinner and thinner tubes, until they are as thin as a silk thread. These tiny tubes, called CAPILLARIES, are small enough to reach into every part of you. Because the walls of these tiny tubes are very thin, the food easily soaks out of the blood, into your muscles, bones, and skin, and everywhere that food is needed. When the food reaches the hungry parts, the blood has made half of the trip.

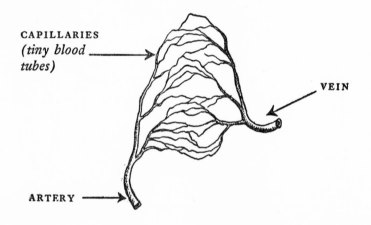

CAPILLARIES
(tiny blood tubes)

VEIN

ARTERY

Now the blood has to make the rest of the trip. The tiny tubes join one another to form thicker and thicker tubes. These tubes, called VEINS, bring blood back to the heart and then to the lungs (you'll find out why later), ready for the next round trip.

In every part of you
—in your arms and in
your legs, in your eyes
and nose, in your fingers,
stomach, knees and toes
—there are blood tubes.
There are large tubes (arteries) bringing in blood,
there are tiny thin-walled
tubes (capillaries) through
which materials seep in
or out, and large tubes
(veins) to carry the blood
back to the heart.

You can't see your
heart, which is tucked
away behind the bones of
your chest. But you can
feel the blood as it pumps
through you. Wherever
your blood tubes run close
to your skin, you can
feel the blood pumping
along.

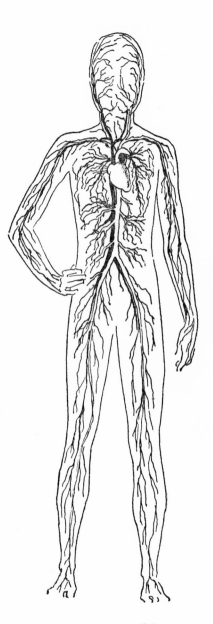

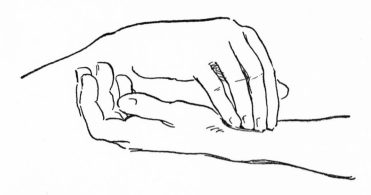

One place where you can feel the beat is at your wrist, about where the picture shows. If you touch your finger-tips to this place, you can feel the beat-beat of the moving blood. This is called feeling your pulse. It is also possible to *see* the moving of your pulse. This is how.

PULSE EXPERIMENT NO. I

You will need: a thumbtack and a paper match.

Try this. Stick the thumbtack into the end of the paper match. Rest the head of the tack on your pulse. You may have to move the tack around a bit until you get the right spot. When you do, you will see the match bobbing back and forth, one bob for each beat of your heart.

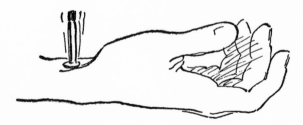

You have felt your heart beat, you have *seen* it beat; now here is something else you can find out about your heart.

PULSE EXPERIMENT NO. 2

TRY THIS. Count your pulse beats for a full minute. This will tell you how fast your heart beats when you are doing an easy job such as reading a book.

NOW TRY THIS. Keep your knees straight, bend over and try to touch your toes. Do this exercise quickly twenty times. Now count your pulse. What happens?

YOU WILL FIND that your pulse is much faster when you're working hard than when you are doing a quiet job.

This is because your body needs more food when it is more active. More food must be rushed to the working parts. Your heart pumps the blood faster and sends it swirling through the liver and the fat layers. Food is picked up and delivered to the hard-working muscles so that they can catch that forward pass, run those bases, or lead the cheers.

Whether you're sleeping or eating, or walking or dancing, your heart pumps just fast enough to take care of the needs of your body.

3. What Your Body Is Made Of

You know that the job of your digestive system is to change the food so that it can be used by your body. You know that the blood carries the digested food to all parts of your body. You know that the heart is a pump that pushes the blood all around your body. You know that there are tubes through which blood flows all around your body. But just what is your body? You know that it's made of skin, muscles, bones, blood, and all kinds of parts both inside and outside. But let's see what these parts of your body are made of. Let's get close to them and take a good look.

Things look quite different when you get close to them. For example, here is the way a brick building looks from a distance.

It's just a small blob on the landscape, isn't it?

Here's what it looks like when you're close to it, a block or so away. You can see that it has walls, doors, and windows.

And here's what it looks like when you're still closer, five feet away. You can see that the walls are made of separate bricks.

Now let's do the same kind of thing, but this time let's look at you instead of at a building.

Here's a picture of your hand as you usually see it. The big circle shows what a small piece of your hand looks like when you hold it close to your eye.

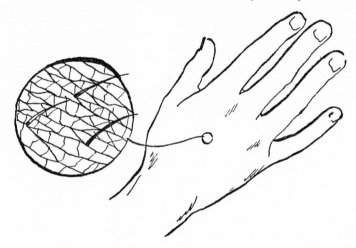

And this is what a very small piece of your skin looks like when you see it through a microscope. The

picture shows a piece of skin about as big as this "o." Notice that the skin is made of separate little pieces. These little pieces are called CELLS.

Your skin isn't the only part of you that is made of cells. Just as the building is made of bricks, every living part of you is made of cells—not only you, but every person, every cat, every bird, every bug, every plant. Every living thing is made of cells. Your whole body is made of cells—cells that come in all shapes and sizes according to the work they do. Here are pictures of a few of the different kinds of cells in your body.

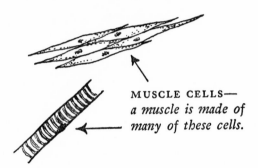

MUSCLE CELLS— *a muscle is made of many of these cells.*

BLOOD CELLS *of several kinds are in your blood.*

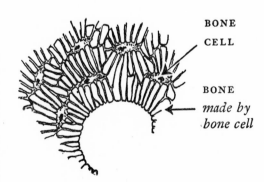

BONE

CELL

BONE *made by bone cell*

FAT CELLS— *many together form layers of fat under your skin.*

37

You are made of billions and billions of living cells. Each one of these cells needs to be fed. And each one is fed, with the digested food that has been brought to it by the blood.

What Cells Do With Food

When the food is in your cells, what happens to it? It doesn't just stay there. It is used by your body in three very important ways:

> Some of the food keeps you growing.
> Some of the food keeps you warm.
> Some of the food keeps you going.

4. Food Keeps You Growing

When you were born, you were about as long as your father's forearm, and you weighed six or seven pounds. Now you're almost as tall as your parents, and you probably weigh more than ten new-born babies. Where did all the extra size and weight come from? From the food you ate, of course. And this is how it happened.

HOW A CELL GROWS

Left: a single cell. Center: the same cell grows and begins to split. Right: the same cell split in two.

When a cell takes in food, it splits in two and becomes two cells. Each one of these cells then takes in food and grows to be full size, and again splits in two. Now there are four cells instead of the one that we started with. And so it is with your bone cells, blood cells, muscle cells, and the other kinds of cells. When they take in food they grow, split and become many cells.

That is how you grow taller and wider and heavier. You now have many more cells than when you were a baby.

When a building is being built, each brick must be put in place to make the building grow taller and wider. But all living things grow because they have cells which take in food and grow into many cells.

Even when you stop growing taller and heavier, your cells keep on growing and splitting. This is necessary because you keep using up cells all the time. All parts of you that keep moving and pumping gradually wear out and have to be replaced. You don't see it happen inside your body, but you have seen it happen on the outside many times.

When you scrape your knee while out roller skating, you scrape off many thousands of skin cells. Within a day or two, all these thousands of cells have been replaced. They are replaced by other cells which take in food, grow, and become many cells. Each one of the new cells was formed by an old cell that took in food, grew, and divided. While you ate your lunch, you scraped away many, many cells from the lining of your cheeks. In a few hours, they were all replaced by new cells. These new cells were all made by old lining cells that grew and divided to make more lining. That time when you accidentally cut your finger, millions of blood cells were lost and thousands of skin cells were destroyed. The blood cells were replaced in a few hours, and the skin cells in a few days.

Every second, day and night, asleep or awake, this growing and dividing of cells goes on. Your cells can grow because *the food you eat keeps them growing*.

5. Food Keeps You Warm

Some of the food you eat is burned in your cells, just like coal is burned in a furnace. You needn't run out to call the fire department. There is no danger from the burning that goes on inside of you. It's a steady, gentle burning that goes on all the time in every cell of your body. This burning is what keeps the inside of your body warm, no matter how cold it is on the outside.

You have your own heating system which usually keeps your body warmer than the air around you. Here's a simple way to see for yourself.

TEMPERATURE EXPERIMENT

YOU WILL NEED: an ordinary household thermometer and yourself.

TRY THIS. First look at the thermometer to see what temperature it shows. It will probably read about 70°. This is the temperature of the air in your room. Now tuck the thermometer in your armpit. Leave it under your arm for two minutes and then see what temperature it shows.

You will find that it will read about 90°.

This shows that your armpit is warmer than the air in your room.

The inside of your body is still warmer, almost 99°. it's warmer because of the burning of food in your cells.

This burning that goes on inside your cells is a slow kind of burning that takes place without flames or sparks or smoke, but it is real burning just the same. The food in your cells is burned and heat is made, just as wood in a campfire is burned and heat is made.

You have probably seen other examples of slow burning without flames, sparks, or smoke. The inside of a pile of rotting leaves or grass is warm because of the slow burning that is going on. In cold climates gardeners spread leaves and grass around their berry plants in the fall. The slow burning of the covering helps to keep the roots of the plants warm during the cold winter. In the same way, the slow burning of food keeps you warm on a cold winter day.

More Heat Than You Need

On some days the slow burning in your cells makes more heat than you need. On a hot summer day, for example, the air may be warmer than the inside of your body. You need a cooling system to keep your body from becoming too hot. And you have your own cooling system. The SWEAT GLANDS in your skin act as your private cooling system.

You have millions of these sweat glands located in almost every part of your skin. You sweat, or perspire, through your sweat glands. Each gland takes water (and some liquid waste material) out of your blood and pushes it to the surface of the skin through an opening called a PORE. But how does this make you feel cooler? Here's a way to find out.

44

You will need: a small piece of absorbent cotton dipped in warm water.

Try this. Dab the wet cotton on your wrists. What happens?

You will find that your wrists will feel cool as soon as the water dries away or evaporates from your skin.

When water evaporates, it cools the thing it touches. The water on your wrist evaporated and it cooled the skin it was touching. In the same way, when the sweat glands push water out of your pores, the water evaporates and cools your skin.

That's a pretty useful arrangement, don't you think? And there's even more to it than that. The sweat glands regulate their work according to the weather. On a hot day, they open wide, sending out lots of water to evaporate and cool your skin. You perspire more in hot weather. You feel thirsty on hot days because of all the water that is being lost out of you through evaporation.

On a cold day, the sweat glands close up almost entirely, in order to save the heat being made by the burning of food in your cells.

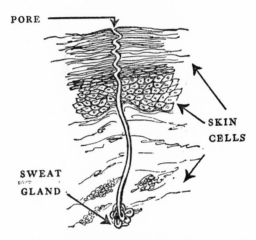

PORE

SKIN CELLS

SWEAT GLAND

SWEAT GLAND, GREATLY ENLARGED

Sometimes the burning in your cells makes entirely too much heat. Then the inside of your body becomes too warm. This sometimes happens when you are sick, and it's called having a FEVER. If the doctor thinks the fever should be cooled down, he does several things to help you cool your body. He tells you to stay in bed and rest. You feel cooler when you lie still than when you are moving about. He tells you to drink lots of liquids, so that your sweat glands will have plenty of water to evaporate. Sometimes you get an alcohol sponge bath. This is a good way to cool your body. Here's an experiment to show why.

COOLING EXPERIMENT NO. 2

YOU WILL NEED: two small pieces of absorbent cotton and a little rubbing alcohol.

TRY THIS. Dip one piece of cotton in water and the other piece in rubbing alcohol. Dab the cotton with the water on it on your wrist. See how long it takes to evaporate, and feel how much it cools your wrist.

Then dab the cotton containing the alcohol on your wrist. Again see how long it takes to evaporate and how much it cools your skin.

YOU WILL FIND that the alcohol evaporates much faster than the water. Because it evaporates faster, it cools your skin faster. That's why an alcohol sponge bath cools a fever so quickly.

Most of the time your body needs no help in keeping you at the right temperature. Whether you are climbing a banana tree in Africa, or fishing through the ice in Alaska, your healthy body stays at the same comfortable temperature. On hot days your sweat glands open wide to send out more water to evaporate and keep you cool. On cold days they close up to save the heat. On all days the cells in your body keep burning food and the burning of the food keeps you warm.

And now you can understand the reason for something else that happens to you once in a while. When you feel very cold, your muscles start to move on their own and you shiver. To make these quick movements your muscle cells must burn lots of food. Burning lots of food makes heat. The heat makes you warm. So you see that when you feel cold, shivering makes heat to help you get warm.

You can't see the slow burning that keeps you warm, but you can feel the results of it every time you exercise or do a piece of heavy work. Do some rapid knee-bending or fast running for two minutes. Now touch your forehead and cheeks.

You will find them quite warm and damp. Look in the mirror. You will see that your face is redder than when you started. You feel hot.

The heavy exercise made your muscle cells burn lots of food. All that burning made lots of heat. That's why you feel hotter. All your sweat glands opened up wide so that quick evaporation would cool your body. That's why your face feels damp. The heat of burning also made your blood warmer, so the tiny blood tubes in your skin opened wider. This allowed more blood to flow to your skin, where it could be cooled by the outside air. That's why your cheeks are pink, too. Everything that happened was caused by the burning of the food in your cells.

What Good Is Keeping Warm?

You see, then, that your body has ways of making you warmer when you're too cold, and of cooling you off when you're too warm, so that your inside temperature always remains just about the same, a bit under 99°. This is a very important advantage to you. You can see just how important it is if you think about an animal whose body cannot warm or cool itself. For example, think of a frog.

A frog's body has no arrangements for warming or cooling itself, and the frog is completely controlled by weather. He must make his home where conditions are right. In the hot summer the frog must live near cool ponds or brooks where he can jump in to cool off. But when winter comes, the frog has no way of keeping warm, so he has to go out of business for several months.

If you can get a frog, you can do an interesting, harmless experiment to see how frogs prepare for their winter sleep, or hibernation, when cold sets in. Put the frog into a glass jar containing some mud and about two

inches of water. Place the jar in a basin of ice-water and cracked ice. Stir the ice-water. When the water in the jar has cooled enough, you will see the frog scurry down into the mud and begin to scoop out a sleeping place for the "winter." After he has made himself comfortable, remove the ice-water from the basin and pour warm water into it. Stir again and wait. Soon the frog will wake up and come to the top again, ready to greet the "spring."

Some other animals have to stay out of the heat because they have no cooling systems. Desert snakes, for example, stay in the shade of a rock or cave all through the blazing daytime heat. If they are disturbed, they scurry as fast as possible to the next shady place. If they don't find a shady place, they wriggle about looking for one, until the heat kills them. Because they have no cooling systems, snakes are helpless in the hot sun.

There are many advantages to being a human being and now you know another one. You can live almost anywhere—in the arctic or on the desert—because you have a cooling system in your sweat glands and a heating system in most of your cells.

Food Can't Burn By Itself

Your body is a clever burning machine. It burns food to keep you warm. Other burning machines burn other things. A steam locomotive burns coal. A diesel locomotive burns oil. A car burns gasoline. But before anything can burn, whether it's food or gasoline or coal or oil or any other fuel, there must be something else besides the fuel. You can find out what it is by doing the following experiment:

BURNING EXPERIMENT

YOU WILL NEED: a friend, three short candles, three saucers, and three glass jars of different sizes. (Because of candle drippings, this experiment should be done in the kitchen sink or on a metal tray.)

TRY THIS. Hold a lighted match under one candle. Then press the bottom of the candle against a saucer to make it stick. Now light the candle. Place the largest glass jar, mouth down, over the candle. What happens?

You will find that the candle will burn for a short time and then go out. Since the only thing in the jar was *air*, the candle must have stopped burning when the air was used up. It seems, then, that a candle needs air in order to burn.

Now try this. Stick the bottoms of the other two candles against the saucers, one in each saucer. Wash out the largest jar. Then light all three candles. Cover each candle with a glass jar. Be sure that you cover all the candles at the same time. Here's where you'll need that friend to help.

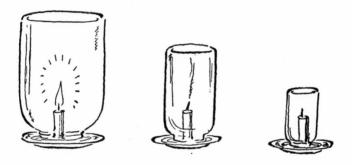

You will find that the candle in the smallest jar will go out first. The candle in the largest jar will be the last to go out. Since the smallest jar has the least air in it, this shows that burning stops when air is used up. Air is necessary for burning.

Actually, air is made of a number of things and only one of them is necessary for burning. This is called OXYGEN, and air has it.

How Oxygen Gets To The Cells

It's easy enough for a candle to get at the oxygen that keeps it burning, because air is all around it. But when burning takes place inside a machine, a special arrangement has to be made to get air to the burning material. In a locomotive, a powerful pump blows air into the burning coal. In the furnace that makes steam for your home or school, there are little doors through which air comes to the burning coal. In an oil burner, an air blower forces air in to the burning oil.

Your body, too, has a special arrangement for bringing oxygen to the cells where food is being burned. You breathe in air all the time. Let's see how the air that you breathe gets to every cell in your body.

You know, of course, that air comes in through your nostrils. In your nose there are small hairs to strain the dust out of the air. Lots of warm blood flows through the lining in your nose. As the air passes the lining, it gets warmed to body temperature by the warm blood. Then the strained, warmed air passes down into

54

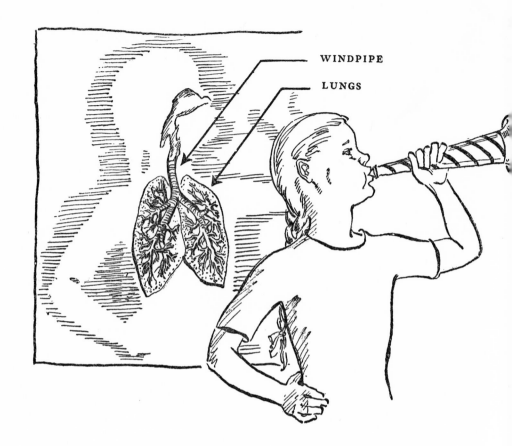

WINDPIPE

LUNGS

a long tube, called the WINDPIPE, which goes down inside your chest. You have two LUNGS so the windpipe divides into two pipes, one for each lung. Inside your lungs the two pipes divide again and again into narrower pipes that branch into every part of your lungs. The air flows through these tubes into every little part of the lungs.

Here's what a small piece of a lung looks like under a microscope. It's full of hollow spaces like sponge rubber. When you breathe *in*, the hollow spaces, called AIR SACS, fill with fresh air.

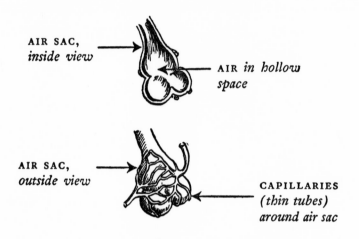

AIR SAC, *inside view*

AIR *in hollow space*

AIR SAC, *outside view*

CAPILLARIES *(thin tubes) around air sac*

Now the fresh air is in the lungs, but how does it get to the rest of the body? Once again, blood is the freight train that carries the goods. Blood flows through tiny tubes that criss-cross around each hollow space of the lungs.

The tiny blood tubes are thin and the walls of the hollow spaces in your lungs are thin. So the air passes right through them into the blood. This blood, as it flows on through your body, has the oxygen that your cells need in order to burn food. The blood, bright red with the oxygen in it, flows from the little tubes around each space in the lungs into larger tubes and larger tubes which bring it to your heart.

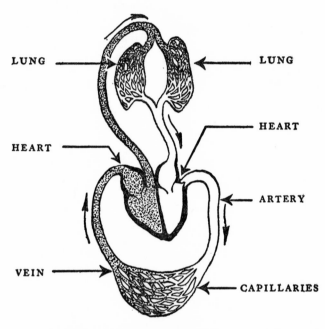

LUNG —   LUNG

HEART —   HEART

ARTERY

VEIN —   CAPILLARIES

DIAGRAM OF BLOOD CIRCULATION

This picture shows only a few of the many arteries, capillaries, and veins in your body.

The heart pumps the blood out through other tubes, called ARTERIES, that branch into smaller and smaller tubes that reach into every place and part of your body. As the blood passes by, each cell takes the oxygen it needs from the blood that flows past it.

As the cells take oxygen out of the blood, it loses its bright red color and turns a darker, bluish shade. Now you can see why some of the blood tubes, called VEINS, like those at your wrist, are bluish. These tubes are carrying blood that has given up its oxygen to the cells. The blood is on its way back to the heart to be pumped to the lungs. There it will pick up a supply of fresh oxygen and turn bright red again.

The Air Pump

Air doesn't just flow into your lungs. It needs to be pumped in and out—and you have two pumps to do it, all the time. The main pump is a curved muscle under the lungs. This curved muscle, called the DIAPHRAGM, is able to move up and down. When it moves up, it pushes air out of the lungs. When it moves down, fresh air flows into the lungs. Your ribs and rib muscles are the other pump.

You don't have to keep telling your breathing muscles what to do or how fast to do it. As you sit quietly, your breathing is slow. If you get up and touch

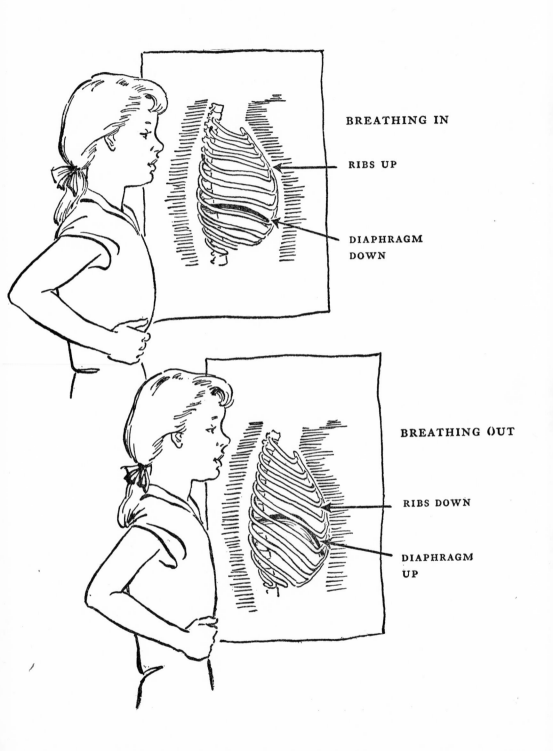

BREATHING IN

RIBS UP

DIAPHRAGM
DOWN

BREATHING OUT

RIBS DOWN

DIAPHRAGM
UP

your toes ten times, you will find that you have to breathe faster.

Of course, you can hold your breath for a short while, but you can't keep it up. There are special parts of you that control your breathing muscles so that your lungs take in the right amount of air for your body's needs without bothering you about it.

Here's a way to feel your ribs at work. Put your hand on your chest and move it down until it touches the bottom ribs. Take a deep breath. You will feel the rib move up to make more room for your lungs to fill up. Now, let the air out. Feel your ribs move down.

When your ribs move down and the curved muscle under your lungs moves up, air is pressed out of the lungs. When your ribs move up and the muscle moves down, fresh air is brought into the lungs.

The air from the lungs, together with the digested food from the intestine, is delivered by the blood to every part of your body. In your cells, the food and the oxygen of the air keep burning to keep you warm.

6. Food Keeps You Going

Next time anyone tells you to sit still, you answer that it can't be done. When you are sitting your very stillest, there is lots of moving going on. Your heart is beating, billions of blood cells are pumping through you, food is being moved along through your stomach and intestine, and many other parts of your body are also moving.

When you walk, run, skip, or ride a bicycle, lots of other parts of you begin to move. Hundreds of muscles get to work moving your arms and legs and fingers and toes and dozens of other parts.

Before all this moving can take place, something has to happen inside your muscle cells. We can't easily see what happens inside your cells. But we can see what happens in other moving things. For example, we can see what happens when a locomotive or an automobile moves.

A steam locomotive can move when coal is burning. The burning coal heats water which turns into steam. The steam pushes against certain parts of the machinery, called pistons, which turn the wheels and move the loco-

61

motive. An automobile moves when gasoline is burned. The burning gasoline pushes pistons that turn the car's wheels. In the locomotive and in the car, something had to be burned to make them move along.

You probably don't own a locomotive that you can tinker with, but here's another way of showing that, when material is burned, it makes heat, which can cause something to move.

HEAT-INTO-POWER EXPERIMENT

YOU WILL NEED: a few tablespoonfuls of popping corn, a corn popper or covered frying pan, and a stove on which to heat the corn.

TRY THIS. With your fingernails, try to tear apart a grain of corn. You will find that it is a very hard job. It takes plenty of pull. Now put all the corn into the popper or covered frying pan and heat it over the fire. Soon the corn will pop open completely. Each grain will turn itself entirely inside out.

NOW TRY THIS. Put the butter and salt on the popcorn and eat it. This doesn't prove anything except that hot popcorn tastes good.

When you tried to pull apart a grain of corn, you saw that plenty of force was needed. Yet when the corn was heated, it popped open quickly. Where did the force that blew it open come from? It came from the heat of the stove. This is how. Each grain of corn has a little bit of water in it. When you heated the corn, the heat changed the water into steam. The steam puffed and pushed so hard that it popped the corn open. So you see that when the fuel in the stove was burned it made a force that could move something. It blew the grains of corn apart.

You, too, have to burn something to make you move along. It is not a hot, popping fire, but you *gently* burn food in your muscle cells all the time. Although scientists don't yet know exactly how the slow burning in your muscles is turned into moving force, they know that it does happen. The slow burning of the food gives your muscles the power to move your arms, legs, head, heart, every moving part of you. Every time that some part of you moves, and that is all the time, it moves because a bit of food has been slowly burned in some of your cells.

If you are throwing a ball, extra food is being burned in your arm muscles. If you are dancing, extra food is being burned in your leg muscles. And all the time, whether you are moving or trying to sit still, food is being burned in the muscles of your heart, your digestive system, and many other places. Even when you are fast asleep, there are muscles at work. Whenever a muscle works, it does so because food is being slowly burned in the cells of the muscles.

Muscles In Action

Your body can make hundreds of different kinds of movements, from lifting your eyebrows to lifting a suitcase. These movements seem very different from each other. Yet all of them are alike in one important way. All the different kinds of movements that your body can make are made by muscles.

Let's see what a muscle is and how it works. All your muscles are made of the same kind of cells—muscle cells. And all muscle cells work in the same way. They *contract*. That is, they tighten up and get shorter.

Here's a picture of your arm muscles and a diagram that shows how these muscles, by contracting and getting shorter, can make your arm move.

64

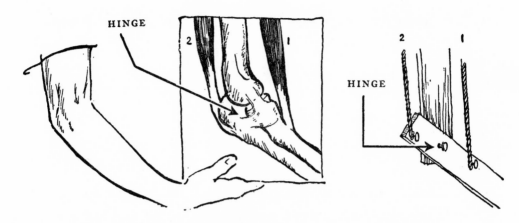

Your arm bones are like the two sticks hinged to each other, and your muscles are like the two cords. When you pull cord number one, the bottom stick moves up at one end. When you pull cord number two, the stick moves down. The muscles work by getting shorter when they receive a signal. When muscle number one receives a signal to get shorter, your forearm goes up. When muscle number two gets the signal to get shorter, your forearm goes down.

The same arrangement of bone and muscle can be found in many places in your body. Your leg and knee, for instance, are connected in almost exactly the same way as your arm and elbow. In other places, such as your neck, there are more than two muscles, and the hinge is made differently, so that you can move your head in many different directions instead of just back and forth.

When you think of all the parts of you that can move, from the waggle of your eyebrows to the wiggle in your toes, you can see that you must have many, many muscles. There's hardly a spot on your skin that you can touch without pressing against some muscle underneath. Most of the fleshy parts of you are really muscles. There are muscles in your arms, your legs, across your back and chest, in your neck. Your face, your eyes, your stomach, all the parts of you that move can do so only because of muscles.

Your moving parts can move in all kinds of ways. They can do all kinds of jobs. The same parts that grab and throw a basketball can thread a tiny needle. Your legs can give a terrific kick to a football, but they can also carry you delicately and quietly on tiptoes, as you sneak out of the house without having made your bed or cleared the table. Your muscles can make your face look angry or sad or happy or puzzled. You can make all kinds of motions that are quick or slow, rough or delicate, simple or complicated, because of the way in which your muscles and bones work together. All this motion is made possible because some of the food you eat is burned in your muscles and your muscles contract.

66

7. Your Body Gets Rid Of Waste

Your body is a food-burning machine. It slowly burns food to keep you warm and to make muscle movements. But all fuel-burning machines have waste materials. If the machine is to go on working properly, these waste materials must be disposed of. What happens to your body's waste materials?

Let's see how another kind of fuel-burning machine —a coal-burning locomotive—gets rid of its waste.

1. The coal that a locomotive burns turns into hot gases. These hot gases are blown out of a smokestack to make room for fresh air. Without fresh air the fire would go out, just as it did in your experiment with the candle and the glass jar.

2. Part of the coal a locomotive uses doesn't burn up completely. Some of it just won't burn. This is the part that is left over as ashes. The locomotive needs to get rid of these ashes to make room for more coal. The ashes drop into an ashpit and the fireman shovels them out of the way.

3. The moving parts of a locomotive gradually wear out. Before new parts can be put in, mechanics have to remove the worn-out parts.

Your body, too, needs to get rid of its waste products for just about the same reasons as a locomotive does.

Waste Gas

When food is burned in your cells, a waste gas is formed. As a matter of fact, it is the same kind of gas that is formed when coal is burned. This gas must be gotten out of the way to make room for fresh air to enter your cells. Again your blood does the carrying. The waste gas passes out of your cells into the blood that flows near every cell. The blood, with the waste gas in it, flows to your lungs. As the blood flows through the tiny veins criss-crossing your lungs, the waste gas passes out of your blood into your lungs. Then, as you breathe out, the gas is pushed up through your windpipe and out of your nostrils.

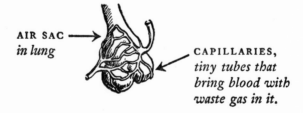

AIR SAC → *in lung*

CAPILLARIES, *tiny tubes that bring blood with waste gas in it.*

Waste Food

The food that you eat is not made entirely of material that your body can use. Some of the food just can't be digested into material that can pass through the walls of the intestine to be used by your cells. Your body can't use the hard, woody parts of vegetables, or the tough, stringy parts of meat, or the hard pieces that your teeth haven't chopped enough. Even though your digestive system has mashed your food, and squeezed it, and poured juices over it, some parts of what you eat just can't be made into things that your body needs. This waste material is moved along through your intestine until it reaches a wider part, called the LARGE INTESTINE.

SMALL INTESTINE

LARGE INTESTINE

The waste material collects at the end of the large intestine. When enough of it has collected, you rid your body of these food wastes in bowel movements.

Worn-Out Parts

Your cells wear out all the time. When you walk, run, jump, even when you sleep, your cells wear out like the parts of a machine. You need to get rid of the worn-out cells in order to make room for fresh cells to grow. Your blood gets to work on this job, too. The waste material of these worn-out cells passes as a liquid into the blood flowing nearby. Some of the waste cell material together with water is pushed out through the pores of your skin when you sweat. But most of it flows along in the blood until it reaches two parts of your

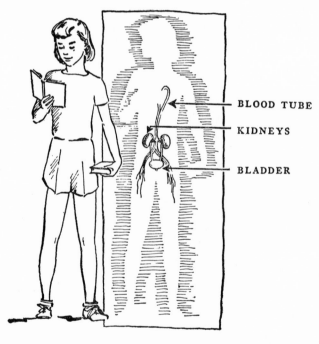

BLOOD TUBE

KIDNEYS

BLADDER

body that look like great big beans. These are called
KIDNEYS.

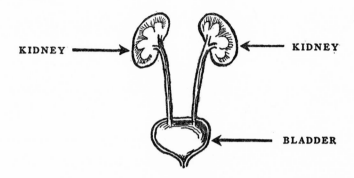

KIDNEY ⟶   ⟵ KIDNEY

⟵ BLADDER

In the kidneys, the waste cell material, together with some water, passes out of the blood into tiny tubes. This water and cell waste make up most of the liquid called URINE. From these tiny tubes in the kidneys the urine flows into two larger tubes. These tubes connect with a muscular bag, called the BLADDER. When a certain amount of urine has flowed through the tubes into the bladder, you can feel it stretching and pressing against the bladder's walls, which tells you that it is time to get rid of this waste material. It flows out through a tube that goes from the bladder to a special opening at the outside of your body.

And now you know how your body does the job of getting rid of the three kinds of waste materials— waste food, waste gas, and worn-out cell materials.

8. Travels Of A Drop Of Blood

By now you can see what a wonderful food-burning machine your body is. It has many different parts that do their special jobs. But none of those parts could do its job if it weren't for the blood. Blood is the freight train that connects with all the parts of the body, bringing them the materials they need and taking away waste.

Let's ride around with a single drop of blood and see the many jobs it does as it flows through your body on its daily rounds. Just follow the numbers in the illustration. Here we go.

1. The drop of blood, together with several thousand others, has just been pumped out of the heart. On this trip, this particular drop flows along until it reaches

2. the tiny tubes in your leg muscles. Here it lets off food and oxygen for the muscles and picks up waste cell material and waste gas. Now it flows through a vein back to another pump in your heart which sends it along to

3. your lungs, where the waste gas is dropped off while fresh oxygen is picked up. Then the drop flows back to another one of your heart pumps, and starts a second trip around your body. This time it goes to

4. your kidneys, where it drops off the waste cell material that

it picked up in the leg muscles, together with some water, forming urine that will be stored in your bladder. Again the drop flows back to your heart, to make another round trip. This time, it goes to

5. the tiny tubes of your intestine, to pick up digested food, and flows on to

6. a leg bone, where the drop leaves some material needed for making bones. On its next trip around, the drop of blood flows to

7. a part of your skin, where it will leave food material and oxygen for your skin cells and pick up waste cell material and waste gas. Then the drop flows to

8. your liver, where it leaves food material to be stored up for future use. A few minutes later, if you start working extra hard, this drop will pick up food from the liver, to be delivered to the rest of your body. On some other trip the drop flows to

9. your stomach muscles, to deliver the food and oxygen that these muscle cells need. At the same time it will pick up waste gas and waste cell material from these muscle cells. On another trip that drop of blood flows into

10. a sweat gland in your skin, where it leaves water and cell waste to be sent out through a pore in your skin.

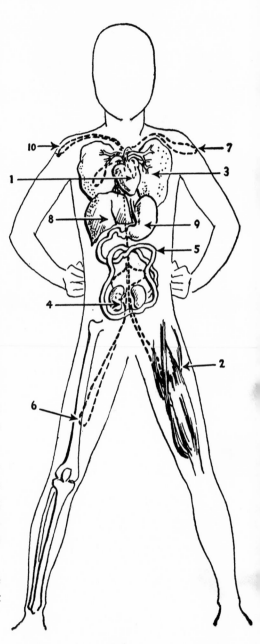

That drop of blood certainly gets around, and so do the millions of other drops that make up the four quarts of blood in your body. A drop of blood is never the same from one second to the next as it flows by your billions of cells. In one place it picks up oxygen and drops off waste gas. In another place it picks up waste gas and drops off oxygen. At still another place it drops off cell wastes, on and on and on, around and around. It makes thousands of round trips every day—more than one every minute—supplying the needs of vast numbers of cells of all kinds and shapes and sizes.

You have a busy drop of blood.

You have a very busy body.

PART TWO
Who's In Charge Here?

1. Your Body Runs Itself

The next time you see a marvelous machine like a jet plane, a streamlined train, or a shiny new car, think how much more marvelous your own body is. Just compare the working of a modern car with the working of your body.

A CAR	YOUR BODY
1. When a car is damaged, someone has to repair it. It can't repair itself.	1. When your body is damaged, it can usually repair itself.
2. When you feed gasoline and oil to a little car, it runs, but it remains little.	2. When you feed a little baby, it grows up to be a full-sized person.
3. A car runs on one special kind of material only — gasoline that has been specially prepared.	3. Your body gets along on many different kinds of food so that each part gets what it needs.
4. A car needs a driver.	4. Your body runs itself.

A machine that can grow, repair itself, and digest its own food is a pretty marvelous machine. But the most marvelous thing of all is that it can run itself. Every second of the day your healthy body regulates itself so that each one of your billions of cells does just the right thing. In your body, there are special cells whose job it is to do the managing. These special cells, called NERVE CELLS, tell the rest of your cells what to do. Let's find out more about them.

It's All Done With Nerve Cells!

"I wonder what's in the package marked 'Do Not Open Until Christmas.'" You are wondering about a package at the same time as you are getting dressed for school. You button each button, tie your shoelaces, and brush your hair, but you never give these jobs a thought. You're too busy wondering about the mysterious box in the closet. Who took care of the getting-dressed job? Nerve cells. And who took care of wondering about the package? Other nerve cells.

Still thinking about Christmas and other important matters, you eat a good breakfast and start out for school. You're still busy thinking when you reach school, but in the meantime you have walked half a mile or so, your stomach muscles have been working on your breakfast, and you stopped for several traffic lights. Who told your leg muscles how to move, and

when to turn right or left? Nerve cells. Who ordered your stomach muscles to get to work? Nerve cells. Who noticed the red lights and told you to wait for the green? Nerve cells.

Everything you do, every second of your life, is controlled by nerve cells. You have billions of them all over your body, in your skin, through each part of you. It's with your nerve cells that you think, and hear, and taste, and smell, and feel happy, and do everything that means being alive. And, when you decide to do something, it's more nerve cells that carry the message to your muscles.

Your nerve cells never stop working. Even when you're fast asleep and perfectly quiet, your nerve cells are busy regulating your heartbeat, controlling your breathing, telling each muscle of your arms and legs to lie still or to shift you to a more comfortable position. While you sleep, other nerve cells keep right on thinking. This kind of sleep-thinking is called dreaming.

Portrait Of A Nerve Cell

Like every other cell in your body, a nerve cell is alive. Like every other cell, it needs food and air. And like every other cell, a slow burning goes on inside it which forms waste materials that must be gotten rid of to make room for fresh food and air.

But in two ways a nerve cell is different from almost any other kind of cell in your body. It's different because of its long, thin shape and because of the way it acts. Its shape is long because it has to carry messages from one part of your body to another part some distance away. A single nerve cell may be so long that it runs all the way from your toe to your head. When one end of it is touched, or warmed, or cooled, or bothered in some way, a sudden change takes place all through the nerve cell. We don't know exactly what the change is, but we do know how fast the message travels. It travels a little over 200 miles an hour, or from one end of a football field to the other (300 feet) in a second. In other words, the message can travel from your toe to your head and back again thirty times in one second.

2. You Can Touch It

Now let's see how nerve cells work for you. Suppose you've just come into the kitchen. On the stove is a pot of delicious-smelling pudding, and in the pot is a spoon. You reach for the spoon, touch it, and ouch! You let go very fast, before you even *know* that the spoon is hot. Now let's see what makes you pull your hand away in such a hurry.

When you touch the hot spoon, the heat bothers a nerve cell in the skin of your fingertip. This is a long nerve cell which stretches all the way from your fingertip up through your arm and shoulder until it reaches your spine, just below your neck. The heat causes a message—"Hot!"—to flash through the nerve cell, all the way from the end of your fingertip to the other end in your spine. There the message is passed along to another nerve cell that stretches from your spine to your arm muscles. The message causes your arm muscles to yank your hand away from the hot spoon.

There are really two parts to the message. The first part, from your fingertip to your spine, says, "Hot." The second part, from your spine to your arm muscles,

82

says, "Take it away in a hurry." At the same time there
is still a third message flashing through a third nerve
cell. This third nerve cell begins in your spine and ends
in your brain. Through this cell comes a message that
says, "Your fingers feel something hot." And this

message causes a large collection of nerve cells in your brain to go into action with all kinds of thoughts. "I wish some people would have more sense than to leave a spoon sticking out of a hot pot. I wonder if I ought to get the burn ointment. I think I'll get another spoon first." And several dozens more.

However, the brain is quite a complicated collection of nerve cells, so we'll leave it for now and come back to it later. Let's stay with the nerve cells in your skin.

When you touched the hot spoon, you knew very quickly that you were touching something hot. A nerve cell told you. A single nerve cell can carry only a single message. But you also knew something else—you knew which finger had touched the hot spoon. That must mean that each finger has its own nerve cell. But you also knew which joint of your finger touched the hot spoon. That shows that each joint has its own nerve cell. You have three joints in each finger, so that means that there are at least three nerve cells to a finger. Do you think your finger has more than three nerve cells? Let's find out.

TOUCH NERVE EXPERIMENT NO. I

YOU WILL NEED: one hairpin, and one friend. You can try this on yourself, but it's more fun with a friend.

TRY THIS. Tell your friend to rest his hand on a table, palm up. Have him turn his head away so that he can't see what you're doing. Ask him to tell you whether he's being touched by one point of the hairpin or two. Hold the points of the hairpin about half an inch apart. Touch his fingertip *lightly* with both points at the same time. What happens?

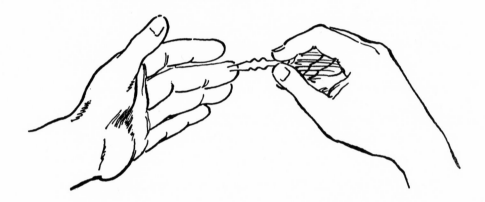

Your friend will say that you are touching him with two points. This means that two separate nerve cells are being touched.

NOW TRY THIS. Bring the points a bit closer and try again. Keep bringing the points closer and closer and keep asking whether you're touching him with one point or with two. What happens?

YOU WILL FIND that when the points are this far apart .. your friend will probably say that you're touching him with one point.

THIS SHOWS that both points are touching the same nerve cell.

NOW TRY THIS. Keep on touching his fingertip, but now start spreading the points apart, a tiny bit at a time. As soon as your friend says "two" you will know that you're touching two separate nerve cells.

THIS SHOWS that the nerve cells in your fingertips are that close together. You have hundreds of nerve cells in each finger.

You need many nerve cells close together in your fingertips because you use your fingers for touching and finding out about things. But do other parts of your body need as many nerve cells? Let's find out.

TOUCH NERVE EXPERIMENT NO. 2

YOU WILL NEED: the same hairpin and the same friend.

TRY THIS. Tell your friend to close his eyes. Touch the inside of his arm with both points of the hairpin, just as you did in the previous experiment. Again ask him to tell you whether he's being touched by one point or two. Find out how close you must hold the points to make him say "one." What happens?

YOU WILL FIND that you can hold the points much farther apart than when you touched his fingertip.

THIS SHOWS that the nerve cells in the arm are

farther apart than the nerve cells in the fingertip. We don't need them as close together because we don't usually touch things with this part of the arm.

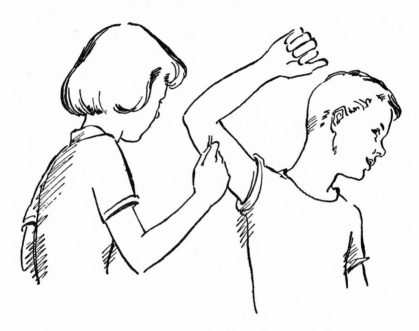

Now try this. Do the same thing in other places —the side of the foot, the lips, the back of the neck, the toes. What happens?

You will find that the places most often used for touching things have nerve cells close together. Other places have nerve cells farther apart.

Here's a way to find out something else about your nerve cells.

You will need: yourself, and a sharpened pencil. The point should not be too sharp.

Try this. On the back of your hand mark off a little square about as big as a postage stamp. Pretend that you're going to fill in this square with dots about as far apart as these dots .. Touch the point of the pencil to each imaginary dot and pay careful attention to what you feel. What happens?

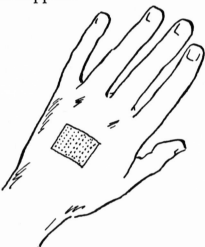

You will find that you don't feel the same thing at each place on your skin. In most places you will feel just the touch of your pencil, but in some places it will feel cold, in other places it will hurt and feel as if the point were much sharper than it really is, and in still other places it will feel hot.

88

THIS SHOWS that different nerve cells send different kinds of messages.

Of course, this isn't a very accurate way of doing an experiment, but scientists who have tried this carefully, many times, believe that your skin has four different kinds of nerve cells, each kind able to send its own message. The four kinds of messages are cold, hot, touch, and pain. When you touched the hot spoon, messages were flashed up through your hot, touch, and pain nerves. If you had touched an ice cube, messages would have been sent through the cold and touch nerves.

If you had touched a piece of "dry ice" which is very much colder than ordinary ice, messages would have been sent through the cold, touch, and pain nerves.

Since every part of your skin has separate nerve cells that feel cold, hot, touch, or pain, you can see that you have plenty of nerve cells. This is about the number you have in your skin: 30,000 cold nerve cells, 250,000 hot nerve cells, 500,000 touch nerve cells, and 4,000,-000 pain nerve cells.

This Won't Hurt A Bit

What would it feel like to be without any pain

nerve cells? In some ways it might be rather pleasant, because nothing could hurt you. Scratches, cuts, burns, bruises, below-zero weather—nothing would bother you in the least. Sounds good, doesn't it? But if you had no pain nerve cells, you could have a bad cut or a dangerous burn, or you could be freezing, and you wouldn't even know it. So you can see that the job of the pain nerve cells is not just to be a nuisance, but to warn you that something harmful is happening to you, and to make you take care of it. Your pain nerve cells give warning of danger.

The nerve cells in your skin tell you about what's touching your skin. Through these cells you learn something about the world around you. Through these cells you feel the cool water in a pool, the warmth of your blankets, the furry feel of your dog, and the sharp warning of a blackberry thorn.

But the sense of touch is only one of the ways of learning about the world around you. You have four other senses—taste, smell, sight, and hearing. And it is through your five senses that the world reaches you with its many messages. Let's find out more about how your senses work for you.

3. You Can Taste It

You found out earlier in this book that the "taste" of apples is mostly smell. Actually you taste most of the food you eat by smell. But you also have a sense of taste. The tasting job is done by nerve cells in your tongue. With these nerve cells, you can receive four kinds of taste messages—sweet, salty, sour, and bitter. And that's all. Everything else that you know about food comes as a smell message.

Each kind of taste message is sent through its own kind of nerve cell. Although the different kinds of nerve cells are located in every part of your tongue, they are not evenly spaced. Some parts of your tongue have a great many sweet nerves and only a few of the others. Some parts have a large number of salt nerves, and so on. Here's a way to find out which parts of your tongue are most sensitive to each taste.

TASTE EXPERIMENT NO. I

You WILL NEED: a pinch of salt, a pinch of sugar, a spoonful of vinegar, and a pinch of bitter-tasting stuff (finely ground coffee will do fairly well for the bitter stuff, but ground-up bitter almonds are better). You will also need a small, clean water-color brush, and a glass of water.

TRY THIS. Dip the brush in water, then touch it to the salt. Touch the wet salty brush to the tip of your

tongue. Does it taste salty? Now, take a sip of water to wash off the salt. Try again, but this time touch the salty brush to the sides of your tongue. Take another sip of water and then try the back of your tongue. What happens?

You will find that the salty taste comes mostly at the tip and sides of your tongue.

Now try this. Test your tongue with each of the other materials. What part of your tongue tastes the vinegar, what part tastes the bitter-tasting stuff, and what part tastes the sugar?

You will find that sour is tasted mostly at the sides, sweet at the tip, and bitter at the back.

Earlier, you learned that saliva helps to digest your food. But it does something else. Here is a way to find out what that is.

TASTE EXPERIMENT NO. 2

You will need: some powdered sugar and a handkerchief.

Try this. With the handkerchief, wipe your tongue dry. Keep your mouth open, so that your tongue will stay dry. Pick up a pinch of sugar and drop it on the tip of your tongue. Do you taste anything? Now close your mouth and moisten your tongue. Do you taste the sugar now?

This shows that sugar must be moist before you can taste it. The same is true of all foods. They can be tasted only if they are moist or wet. Saliva does the moistening job for any dry foods you may eat.

It's A Matter Of Taste

An experiment that was done by a scientist tells part of the reason why some people like certain foods, while others don't like the very same foods. The scientist asked 2,500 people to taste a certain harmless powder. He asked the question, "What does this taste like?" And here are the answers he got: 1,670 people said it tasted bitter, 714 people said it had no taste at all, 59 people said it tasted sour, and 107 people said it had some other taste.

You see, then, that the same thing can taste quite different to different people. It's no wonder that a food which tastes wonderful to you may not taste so good to someone else.

4. You Can Smell It

Another way you have of knowing about the world around you is through your sense of smell.

How would it be to have no sense of smell at all? You don't have to think hard about it. All you have to do is to remember the last time you had a cold. Your nose was clogged up so that smells couldn't get through.

Without a sense of smell you would miss some pleasant things. You couldn't smell the clean, salt sea breeze, or the new hay, or even the barber shop. The good smell of cooking couldn't get through to make your digestive system prepare for the food you were about to eat.

Smell can be an important sense—when we smell smoke, we are warned that there is a fire somewhere near by—but smell is much less important to people than it is to many animals. Your dog, for instance, depends very much on his sense of smell for information on what's happening around him. You can dress up for a Hallowe'en party, with crazy clothes on, and a good mask, or a putty nose, beard, mustache or fancy wig. When you've finished, you feel sure that nobody can recognize you, but as soon as your dog comes near you, he isn't fooled at all. How can he tell so easily who you are?

Your dog has a very fine collection of smell nerves. That's why your disguise didn't fool him for a minute. Your own collection of smell nerves is just so-so, which is why you and your friends can dress up and fool each other and your families. Nearly everything has some kind of smell, and most living things (except plants), have special nerve cells with which to recognize things by their smell.

Your smell nerves behave differently from most of your other nerves in one special way. Do you know what it is? Here's a way to find out.

SMELL EXPERIMENT

YOU WILL NEED: your friend, and something pleasant for her to smell (perfumed soap, vanilla, mint leaves, and most candies have a pleasant smell).

TRY THIS. Blindfold your friend. Tell her that

you're going to hold something pleasant-smelling in front of her nose and that after a while you will take it away. She is to tell you when you have taken it away.

Now DO THIS. Hold it in front of her nose and *keep it there*. Tell your friend to keep sniffing away. What happens?

You WILL FIND that after a while, depending on how strong the smell is, she will tell you that you have taken it away, even though it is still in front of her nose.

THIS SHOWS that smell nerves can recognize smell for only a short while. They get tired very easily.

It's very fortunate that smell nerves do tire easily. Think of what it would be like if they didn't. Nobody could work in a paint factory, or a chemical laboratory, or a cheese factory, or a leather tannery, or any other strong-smelling place. Perhaps you've wondered how gluemakers and sewer-cleaners can stand the smell. Now you know. After the first few minutes these workers don't smell their job.

There are other places, too, where you can be glad that your smell nerves get tired. When you first step into a crowded movie theatre or a poorly ventilated room full of people, the smell is quite strong, but after a few minutes you don't notice it any more. If your smell nerves didn't get tired, you'd have a hard time enjoying the movie or party.

While we're on this smelly subject, can you think of one smell that your smell nerves stopped noticing a long time ago? It's yourself, of course. Your dog recognized you by it, in spite of your Hallowe'en outfit. And since your smell is something like that of your family and friends, you've become used to their smells, too. But sometimes, when you meet a person who comes from a different climate, or who eats different foods, you do notice a smell. Of course, that person also notices a smell—yours.

So you can see that it's good to have a sense of smell, and it's good that the smell nerves get tired easily.

5. You Can See It

Perhaps the most important way you know about the world is through your sense of sight. Through your eyes you have learned about night and day, far and near, light and shadow. The stars you can never touch can be seen. The lights on a Christmas tree, the flash of lightning, the rainbow, the way your friends look, the color of your clothes, many of the things that make the world such an interesting place come to us as sight messages. You know what it is like to be without sight from being blindfolded in party games or walking in the dark, but did you know that there was a time when you couldn't "see?" You don't remember it, but this is what your mother looked like to you when you were two days old, a week old, and two months old.

2 DAYS OLD   **1 WEEK OLD**   **2 MONTHS OLD**

99

During your first month, your eyes were busy learning to see. It wasn't easy, because many different parts of you had different jobs to learn. These many parts must have learned their jobs quite well, for here you are, busily reading, and that's about the most skilled job that a pair of eyes can do.

Let's find out about the different parts of the eye, starting with the outside. Each eye is called an EYEBALL because it's almost perfectly round, like a ball. To the outside of each eye are attached six muscles. The six muscles move each eye so that it looks wherever you want it to. For instance, to look toward the left, the left muscle of each eyeball pulls it to the left. In the same way, the other muscles pull your eyes toward the right, up, down, or even round and round.

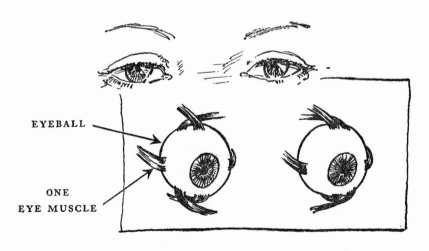

EYEBALL

ONE
EYE MUSCLE

Now let's see what happens inside the eyeballs. Of course, you can't really look inside your eye, but you *can* do an experiment that will tell you a great deal about how you see. For this experiment, you will have to take some time and trouble, but it's really worth doing because the results are very interesting.

SIGHT EXPERIMENT NO. I

YOU WILL NEED: a sheet of white paper about the size of this page, and a sheet of cardboard or heavy wrapping paper about as wide as the window in your room and about eight inches high. You will also need a magnifying glass or lens which is a round piece of glass thicker in the center than at the edges. You can usually get one at the five-and-ten or at a stationery store. (This experiment works best in a room that faces a sunny street, and that can be well darkened.)

TRY THIS. Cut a hole the size of your magnifying glass in the paper. Make the room as dark as you can by pulling the shades, but at the window that faces the sunny street, leave the shade about eight inches high above the window sill. Fasten the cardboard with the hole in it in this space with tacks or scotch tape. Now you are ready for the first part of your experiment.

Hold the sheet of white paper a few inches behind the hole. You'll see a circle of light on the white paper, and that's all you will see. The light from the street came through the hole and made a circle of light on the paper. Nothing very surprising so far.

CIRCLE OF
LIGHT ON
THE PAPER

Now try this. With one hand hold the magnifying glass so that it fits into the hole in the cardboard. With the other hand, hold the white paper against the magnifying glass. Then slowly, slowly, move the paper away. When the paper is just the right distance away (the right distance depends on the shape of your magnifying glass) a surprising thing will happen. What do you see?

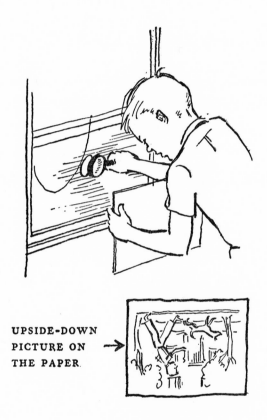

UPSIDE-DOWN PICTURE ON THE PAPER. →

YOU WILL FIND that a small colored picture of the street outside will show up on the white paper. This will not be an ordinary color picture, like the ones you see in a magazine. This will be a living picture, with people walking, cars riding along, everything that's happening outside. What's more, the picture will be upside down—the house across the street upside down, people walking upside down, cars riding upside down.

THIS SHOWS two things. When light comes through a plain hole, it just makes a circle of light where it strikes. When it comes through a magnifying glass, the light forms an actual picture upside down.

How Your Eyes Work

You have two magnifying glasses called LENSES, one in each eye. They are near the front, made of clear transparent cells. They are the black-looking centers of your eyes. They look black because when you look *at* them, you're really looking *through* them into the dark insides of your eyeballs. It's the same as when you look at the window of a darkened room. The window will seem black because you are looking through it into the dark inside of the room.

In your experiment with the magnifying glass, a picture was formed on the white sheet of paper. In your eye, a lens forms a picture on the RETINA or back of your eyeball. The back of the eyeball is filled with hundreds of thousands of nerve cells of a very unusual

104

kind. They are unusual because, when light shines upon them, they send a message. Each little nerve cell gets a tiny part of the picture and then sends its own message to the brain. In the brain all the little messages are added together into something which means that you can see.

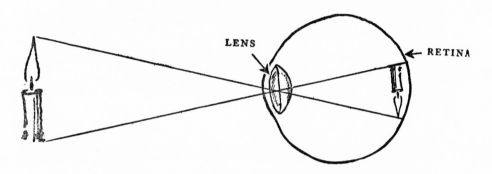

LENS

← RETINA

And that isn't all. If your lens were made of glass, you would be able to see clearly only the things that were a certain distance from your eye. Anything close and anything farther away would look blurry like the picture on the paper looked until you got the lens the right distance from it. Your eye lenses are not made of glass, but of soft living cells whose shape can be changed. Tiny muscles attached to the lens take care of changing its shape so that it always forms a clear picture on the back of the eyeball. When you look at something far away, the lens is pulled into a long, thin shape. When you look at things nearer and nearer to you, the lens is squeezed into a shorter, rounded shape.

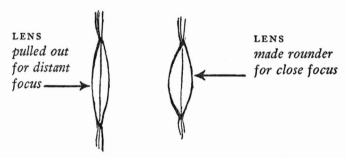

LENS
*pulled out
for distant
focus* ——➤

LENS
*made rounder
for close focus* ←——

Changing the shape of the lenses makes it possible for you to focus your eyes on objects at different distances and get a clear picture at each distance.

Just Enough Light

If each eye had only a lens, lens muscles, and nerves at the back of the eyeball, you would be in trouble. The nerve cells in the back of the eyeball can't stand a bright light. They get stunned by it, and stop sending messages altogether for a few seconds or even longer. That's why, when you look at a very bright light, and then turn away, you can't see anything for a while. (Don't do it, it's not good for your eyes.) So you need some sort of arrangement that will keep too much light from coming in on a bright day, and yet will allow as much light as possible to come in on a gloomy day or in a dark place. You need something like a pair of window shades that can be pulled down when the light is too bright.

In each eye you have such a window shade—the colored part of the eye. It is called the IRIS and is made up of many tiny muscles. These muscles are controlled by nerve cells which automatically regulate the size of the opening in the eye to the amount of light. Also they are arranged so that they always leave a round hole for the light to come through.

You can see these window shades at work, opening up in dim light and closing down in bright light, if you do this experiment.

SIGHT EXPERIMENT NO. 2

YOU WILL NEED: yourself, a place with dim light, a mirror, and a lamp with the shade off (or a flashlight).

TRY THIS. Have the lamp in front of you, with the light turned off. Look at your eyes in the mirror, and notice the size of the black transparent lens, and of the colored iris of the eye. Keep looking at the black part and turn the light on. What happens?

YOU WILL FIND that the colored iris closes in, so that the black hole in the center gets smaller. This lets less light get through into the eyeball. Turn out the light, and the opposite will happen, allowing more light to get in.

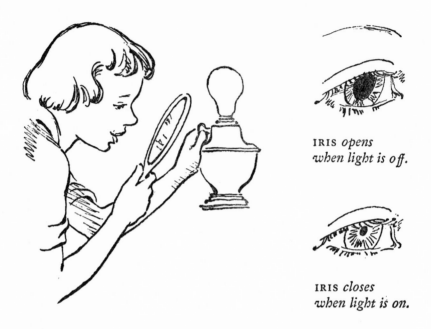

IRIS *opens when light is off.*

IRIS *closes when light is on.*

You may have noticed that the colored part of the eye closes down much faster than it opens up. That's because it's more important to protect the nerves at the back of the eyeball quickly in bright light than it is for them to open up in dim light. This explains something that happens to you when you come into a dark place like a movie theatre on a bright day. The theatre seems very dark, and you can't see your way to a seat for quite a while. When you came in from the outside, the irises of your eyes were shut down to tiny openings, to protect your eyes from the bright sunshine. It took them quite a few seconds to open up as wide as is necessary to see in a place as dimly lighted as a movie theatre.

Why Two Eyes?

Why do you have two eyes? Here's an experiment that will show you why two eyes are better than one.

SIGHT EXPERIMENT NO. 3

You will need: yourself and a fountain pen.

Try this. Hold the cap of the pen in one hand. Hold the rest of the fountain pen, point up, in the other hand with your arm stretched almost straight out. Close one eye. Try to put the cap on the pen in one quick movement. What happens? Try again.

You will find that sometimes you will bring

the cap too near and sometimes too far. It's hard to judge distance with one eye.

Now try the experiment with both eyes open. You won't have any trouble capping the pen.

THIS SHOWS that it is easier to judge distance with two eyes.

Filling In The Picture

The nerve cells of the retina at the back of the eyeball are not packed tightly next to each other. There are spaces between each nerve cell and the next to allow room for fresh food and air to come in, and for waste materials to be removed. Because of these spaces that have no nerve cells, your brain really receives messages that are like a collection of dots, with spaces in between. For instance, when you look at a dog, your eye nerves send a collection of dot messages like this to your brain.

In your experiment with the lens you saw that the picture on the paper was upside down. In your eyes, too, the picture is formed upside down. But your brain turns the picture over so that you see it right side up. Your brain also fills in the spaces between the dots so that you can see the whole picture.

Reading these words seems like a very simple thing, but just think of all the separate jobs that are going on.

1. Tiny lens muscles are busy shaping each lens so that it forms a clear picture at the back of each eye.

2. Tiny iris muscles are busy regulating the size of the eye openings so that just the right amount of light goes in.

3. Still other muscles are busy turning your eyes from left to right and back again, as you read each line.

4. Your brain fills in the dots and turns the picture right side up.

There is no camera, no telescope, or microscope as cleverly built or as useful as your own two eyes.

6. You Can Hear It

Imagine what it would be like to live in a perfectly soundless world—no voices, no laughter, no music, none of the thousands of familiar everyday sounds like footsteps on the stairs or the far-off whistle of a train—just endless silence. That will give you some idea of how much you depend on your ears for all kinds of information about what goes on around you.

How Sounds Are Made

You can find out something about how you make sounds by holding your thumb and finger against the front of your throat. Now make a deep growling sound, like a bear whose pocket has just been picked. You will feel a slight buzzing in your fingers. This buzzing came from inside your throat, in the VOICE BOX. You make sounds with your voice box.

The buzzing was made by two thin, flat sheets, called VOCAL CORDS. When you blow air between these two sheets, they shake rapidly back and forth, or vibrate. That's the buzzing you felt in your fingers.

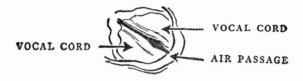

How Sounds Are Heard

The buzzing, vibrating, vocal cords cause the air in the room to vibrate, too. The vibrating air strikes a part of the ear called the EARDRUM. This makes the eardrum vibrate. The vibration is passed along through three little bones to a snail-shaped tube, called the COCHLEA, filled with liquid. Touching the liquid there are several thousand nerve cells, each one connected

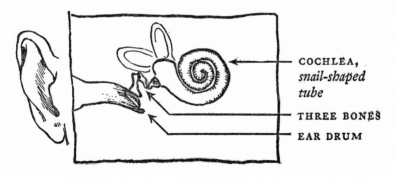

to your brain. When a sound makes the liquid vibrate, the liquid causes the nerve cells to vibrate and send messages to your brain.

Which Side Is Up?

Besides hearing sounds, your ears do another job for you. Here's how you can find out what this job is.

ROCKING CHAIR EXPERIMENT

You will need: a friend and a rocking chair or swing.

Try this. Blindfold your friend and have him sit in the chair. Rock him back and forth very slowly several times. Then stop when he is all the way back. Ask him to tell you what position he is in.

You will find that he can tell you pretty exactly.

There's nothing amazing about this until you stop to ask yourself how anybody can know the position of his body when he is blindfolded. He can't see, yet he knows. What part of his body told him?

The answer lies in three little curved tubes above each snail-shaped hearing tube. These little curved tubes are filled with liquid and each has a clump of nerve cells at the bottom. When you tip your head in any direction, the liquid presses harder against some of the nerve cells than against the others. All the nerve cells send messages to your brain, but the ones that feel the stronger pressure send a stronger message.

That's how you know that you are tipped way back in the rocking chair. When your head is straight up, all three clumps of nerve cells send the same message and that tells you that your head is upright. So you see that two important kinds of messages come through your ears—messages of balance and messages of sound.

7. You Can Figure It Out

Let's take a rest for a while. You've been quite busy learning about the parts of your body. Perhaps you are beginning to think that your body is just a collection of wonderful parts. That's why it may be a good idea to stop for a moment and think about you as a whole person.

The country is a pleasant place for resting and thinking. It's summer time, and you're lying on the grass looking up at the sky, feeling lazy and dreamy. The clouds make strange imaginary shapes as you watch them. You see a tiny moving spot high up in the clouds. It might be an airplane, but, as it comes down lower, it turns out to be a hawk, gliding slowly in great, lazy circles.

By turning your head a bit, you can see smoky blue hills far away, and closer to you, a clump of white birch trees. Still closer to you, a black-and-yellow butterfly glides in for a landing on a leaf. As you watch it slowly opening and closing its wings, you see something pinkish and brown moving along in the earth, under the leaf.

It's a moist, shiny earthworm, moving along at top

speed, for an earthworm. You look at it and wonder—
does the earthworm know that this is a perfect day for
being lazy? Can an earthworm feel happy about white
clouds and blue hills? What does the world feel like
to an earthworm?

To an earthworm, with no eyes and no ears, the
world is a dark place of no size, no space, no color and
no sound. To an earthworm, being alive means just the
touch and taste and smell of earth and pebbles and grass.
You could almost say that there is no world for an
earthworm, only the things that touch its skin. Not
much fun, being an earthworm.

How about the hawk, with its sharp eyes and sensitive ears? Does the hawk know that this is a wonderful
day for being lazy and dreamy? Can a hawk feel happy
about gliding hour after hour over high blue hills and
sunny fields? What does the world feel like to a hawk?

The world is a much bigger place to a hawk than it is to an earthworm. Soaring high up among the clouds, he can see for miles and miles. He can see the blue hills that you see, and he can also see the little lake beyond the hills, and some tiny white houses, and a tiny train puffing through a shady valley. With his sensitive ears he can hear the swish of his wings cutting through the air, and the puffing and clanging of the tiny locomotive miles away. As you watch him you think to yourself, "I wish I could be a hawk for just one day!"

But you don't really mean that. What you really mean to say is, "I wish I could be myself in a hawk's body for just one day." Because being a hawk means other things besides gliding silently high above the world. It means *not knowing* how wonderful it is to be able to fly. It means not knowing that blue hills and tiny white houses are beautiful. It means not being glad that today is warm and sunny, because a hawk can't remember that yesterday was cold and rainy. It means knowing only about *now*, and never knowing that there was once a yesterday and that there will be a tomorrow. Not much fun, being a hawk, after all.

A radio comedian thought he was being funny when he said, "People have more fun than anybody," but it's

118

very, very true. It's true because people are the only living things that have senses that bring them messages from the outside world *and* a brain clever enough to understand and remember and enjoy the messages that come in. Through your eyes, ears, nose, mouth, and skin the world comes to *you*. Everything that you know, and everything that you will ever learn, comes to you through your five senses. It's because you have these senses *and* a clever brain working together for you that the world is such a wonderful place.

What Makes You, You?

There are more than two billion people in this world. That's a big number. If you could keep on counting, one-two-three-four, and so on, night and day, it would take you sixty years to count two billion! There are so many people in the world and yet, in all that two billion, there isn't a single person who is exactly like you.

When some one says that he likes you, what *you* is he really talking about? Is it the hundred pounds or so of living cells of which you're made? Of course not. He likes you for the way you do things, the way you think, the way you feel about things. He likes you because you can take a joke, because you share things fairly, because he and you may have the same hobbies.

You get along fine, but you and he are not exactly alike. There is nobody in the whole world who thinks and feels exactly like you. You are a very special person.

In what part of you does this special *you* live? Not in your stomach or bones or skin. These parts don't make the difference. It's your brain that makes you not exactly like anybody else. It's with your brain that you enjoy fishing, or like to read adventure stories, or don't like certain kinds of cheese. It's with your brain that you have learned to understand English, or to write letters. It's your brain that remembers the date of Christmas and forgets the capital of Chile. It's with your brain that you are different from other human beings in many ways, and it's also with your brain that you and they are alike in many ways.

8. How Your Brain Works

When a scientist looks at a tiny piece of brain, he doesn't see dates, or a liking for fishing, or a dislike of cheese. He sees something that looks like this.

BRAIN CELLS THROUGH A MICROSCOPE

Your entire brain is made up of billions of nerve cells, together with other cells that bring fresh food and air to the nerve cells, and take away waste materials. The billions of nerve cells aren't just crammed any old way inside your head. They are tucked away safely in the hollow space of your bony skull, and they are arranged in three separate parts, or departments.

Each department has its own set of special jobs to do. Many jobs are shared by the three departments, and no single department can work entirely by itself. However, each department of your brain is in charge of its own special set of jobs. Let's call these three departments the Thinking Department, the Action Department, and the Pumping Department.

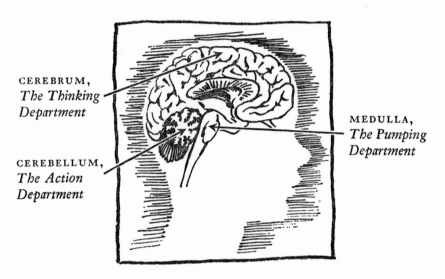

CEREBRUM, *The Thinking Department*

CEREBELLUM, *The Action Department*

MEDULLA, *The Pumping Department*

The Thinking Department

Your Thinking Department is the part of you that learns, remembers, forgets, likes, dislikes, feels happy or sad, knows about smell, taste, feeling, seeing, and hearing. It's the part that tells your legs to take a walk, or decides to go to the movies. You are much brighter than a dog because you have a much bigger and better Thinking Department. You are much, much, brighter than an earthworm, because an earthworm has no Thinking Department at all. It's with this part of your brain that you have been reading these words and thinking about them. It's your Thinking Department that will make you obey or disobey any command.

Raise your hand.

Did you obey the command? If not, please do, so that we can go ahead. Now let's find out what happened.

When you looked at the command, millions of nerve cells went to work. And this is what they did.

1. A little picture of the words, "Raise your hand," was formed at the back of each eye. Here nerve cells received the picture of these black lines on white paper and sent it along to a special place in your Thinking Department.

2. In this special place, other nerve cells received the picture and saw it as black, wiggly lines. To these nerve cells it didn't mean any more than 舉起你的手 which says "Raise your hand" in Chinese. The nerve cells then flashed the picture to another part of your Thinking Department.

3. In this part, other nerve cells received the "Raise your hand" picture and made sense out of it. They

understood it because when you were younger these nerve cells learned to read. That is, they learned to make meaning out of the wiggly lines called the letters of the alphabet. From this reading section of the Thinking Department a message whizzed along to still another section in the same department.

4. In this section the message was received by nerve cells, which set off other little messages, like "Why should I do what the book tells me to? Oh well, it can't hurt me to raise my hand. All right, I'll do it." As soon as the "I'll do it" part happened, a message was sent to another section, still in the Thinking Department.

5. This section has nerve cells that can send commands to the muscles of your arms, legs, neck, toes, fingers, and every part of you that can take orders. A message was sent from the Thinking Department through the nerves leading to your arm muscles. This message commanded your arm muscles to move, and your hand rose.

All this happened in a flash, even though it took more than two hundred words to describe it in the very simplest way. Actually, there were many more steps between seeing the words and doing what they said. There were many more messages, too. Perhaps

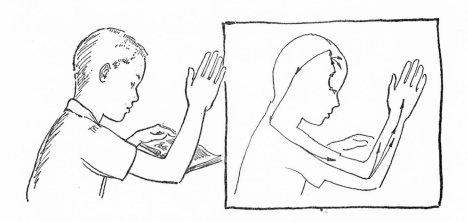

these were some of them: "Shall I raise my right hand or my left?" "Today at school I raised my hand when I knew the right answer." "In that mystery program I heard on the radio today, the court clerk said, 'Raise your right hand and repeat after me . . .'"

Even when you think a very simple thought, like "I'm hungry," you have set to work hundreds of thousands of nerve cells in the Thinking Department of your brain. The Thinking Department is such a complicated collection of nerve cells that nobody in the world knows everything about it. But every time a scientist does find out something new about this part of the brain, it seems even more astounding. For example, scientists have calculated the number of nerve cells in the Thinking Department. The number is more than ninety billion. We are talking of nerve cells only. There are many other kinds of cells in this part of the brain. Yet if you could pack together all these ninety billion nerve cells, they would fit into an empty walnut shell!

Just think of it—everything you ever learned from the time you were born until this second, everything you will learn at school and everywhere else during the rest of your life, everything you know how to do, everything that makes you *yourself* and not anybody else in the world, everything you feel and think about— all this is in a collection of nerve cells that could fit into a walnut shell!

All the most marvelous inventions, books, music, pictures, and ideas in the world come out of the Thinking Department of the brain. But there is no invention one-thousandth as marvelous as your Thinking Department.

The Action Department

Suppose that when you visited a big automobile factory you found the chief engineer wrapping up box lunches in the cafeteria. Wouldn't you think it rather silly and wasteful for a man who can do special work to be doing a job that many other people can do as well or perhaps better? The chief engineer has his own thinking and planning job to do. He was hired for that job because he can do it well. It's wasteful for him to spend his time wrapping lunches.

The chief engineer of You & Company is your Thinking Department, that part of your brain that makes all the decisions, does all the thinking, gives most of the commands, does most of the learning, and takes all of the responsibility. Your Thinking Department has a big job, and it's important that it shouldn't be bothered with other jobs at the same time.

For example, right at this moment you are busy changing these black marks on the page into words and understanding these words. Suppose that at the same time you had to keep thinking about other jobs, such as sitting up in your chair, or breathing, or telling your heart to keep beating, or digesting your meal. You wouldn't be able to pay much attention to your reading. That's why your body has many assistant engineers, foremen, and workers, all of them busy running your body's machinery.

It's hard to say which of these helpers is the most important, but certainly one of the most important is a collection of nerve cells that can be called the Action Department. The Action Department takes charge of the orders sent to your muscles by your Thinking Department. When you raised your hand, the Action Department directed the motion of your arm muscles so that the motion was smooth and easy, instead of being jerky like the motions of a three-month-old baby.

Right now, this section of your brain is telling the muscles in your back to keep you sitting up, and telling the muscles in your arms to hold the book. This spares your Thinking Department the trouble of paying attention to these jobs. You wouldn't get much reading done if, every time you became interested in the book, your back slumped over, you dropped the book, and your chin hit the floor with an awful whack. Reading a book seems like rather quiet work, and yet your Action Department has plenty to take care of.

You weren't born with an Action Department all trained and ready to go. As a baby, you had to *learn* to pick up a rattle, to sit straight, to walk. Right now, if you're learning to dance, it's your Action Department that's doing a lot of the learning. In the meantime, your Thinking Department is sending the directions "right foot slide, bring up left foot, keep off partner's feet." When you get to a point where you can dance and make charming conversation at the same time, you can thank your Action Department for

128

having learned to take care of your feet, leaving your Thinking Department free to think up clever remarks like "Hot, isn't it?"

Assistants Along The Line

However, there are other local jobs to be done, and there are other nerve cells to do them. For example, the muscles of your stomach and intestine have to be told to churn the food and to move it along. For this job, there are several clumps of nerve cells—assistants along the line. Some are located near your back, and others are close to the parts that they control. There are assistants to take care of your liver, your blood tubes, and many other parts whose work must go on without your attention.

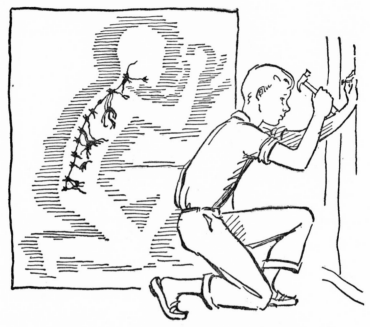

ASSISTANTS ALONG THE LINE (GANGLIA)

The Pumping Department

Whether you're dancing, or playing football, or sleeping, there are two jobs that must go on every second of the day and night. Blood must be pumped throughout your body and air must be pumped into and out of your lungs. These two jobs are so important that a special group of cells, the Pumping Department, is set aside to do almost nothing else but send messages all the time to your heart muscles and to your breathing muscles.

The Spinal Cord

The three main departments of your brain receive and answer messages from all over your body. The brain is pretty far away from many of these places. For instance, when you stand on a diving board and feel for the end of it with your toe, the message must travel from your toe all the way up to your brain in order for you to know about it. The "You're at the end now, stop!" message must travel from your brain back to your leg muscles.

In the same way, all the millions of nerve cells in your skin send their messages of touch, hot, cold, and pain all the way to your brain. And many hundreds of muscles must receive messages of command from your brain in order to do their jobs.

All these messages, zipping back and forth between your brain and the rest of you, have a special well-protected cable through which to travel. This cable is

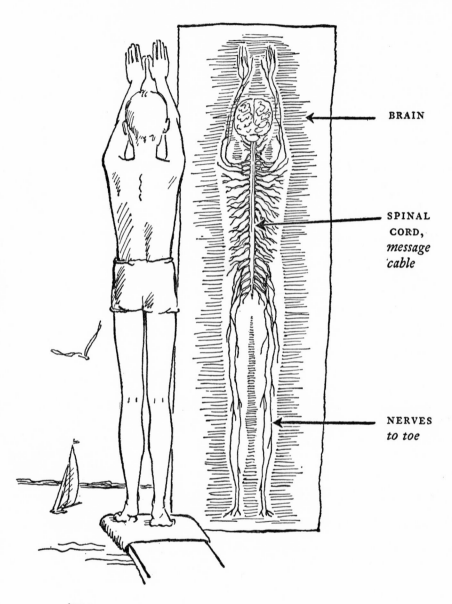

BRAIN

SPINAL
CORD,
*message
cable*

NERVES
to toe

inside your hard, bony spine. It is called the SPINAL CORD.

Your spinal cord consists of a great many long, thin nerve cells, lying side by side, safely protected inside your backbone, or spine. These long, thin nerve cells are of two kinds. One kind carries messages from your skin and other parts of you to your brain. The other kind carries messages from your brain to all the parts of you that your brain can command. Each nerve cell connects one tiny part of your body with one or more nerve cells in your brain or in your spine.

There are more than four million pain nerve cells lying side by side in your spinal cord, and each one has its own nerve connection to the brain. Besides these, there are the hot, cold, and touch nerve cells. And, of course, there are the hundreds of muscles all over your body which get their orders from the brain through the long nerve cells in the spinal cord. All these nerve cells must be very thin if so many of them fit inside your spine.

They are so thin that you could thread 100,000 nerve cells together through the eye of an ordinary needle! Yet, thin as they are, each cell carries its own message, and the messages never get crossed.

Your Brain At Work

Think how very busy your brain must be in such an active job as playing football. Suppose you're ten yards from the goal posts and you've got the ball. A tackle is coming in on you from the left, one of your own team is yelling for you to pass the ball to him. Should you dodge, or pass the ball, or try for a touchdown? Whatever decision you make has to be made by your chief engineer, your Thinking Department. In the meantime, your Action Department has helped to keep your legs moving straight ahead, as fast as possible, your arm muscles holding on to the ball, and a lot of other big and little muscles working together. At the same time, your Pumping Department has kept your heart pumping blood and your breathing muscles pumping air. If you scored that touchdown, it was the teamwork of all the parts of your brain controlling your body, that made it possible.

9. Liquids That Give Orders

Look at yourself in the mirror. Count to ten, and then look again. Do you look any different before and after you started counting? You can't see any difference, and yet while you were counting many changes took place in your body.

Your bone cells made some hard white material, so that your bones are a bit longer and wider than when you started counting.

Your skin cells grew and divided so that you have a little more skin than you did a few seconds ago.

In the soft center of your bones several million new blood cells were made.

And many other changes took place while you were looking at the mirror. All together these changes are what people call growing.

While you counted to ten, you grew, but your parents did not. What made it happen to you, but not to them? Who sent the orders to your cells, but not to theirs?

Growing

The growing orders came from a small clump of cells under your brain, called a GLAND. You have many glands in your body, but this one is especially important. Out of the food it gets, this gland makes tiny amounts of a special liquid that enters your blood and is carried to all parts of your body. This special liquid makes your cells grow. And every few months you need larger shoes or longer skirts or the next size jacket. The growing orders keep coming to your cells and you keep right on growing until you've grown to your full size. This usually happens in your twenties. At your full size the gland under your brain stops making its special liquid and, though you may get fatter, you stop growing taller.

This way of sending orders is quite different from the way the nerve cells do the job. A nerve cell flashes its order directly from one place to another. The nerve cells in your nose can carry the good news of chocolate cake only to your brain. But the drops of liquid that bring the grow order are carried by your blood to all parts of your body. Such an order-carrying liquid is called a HORMONE. In your blood there are many different hormones. Each one is made by its

GROWING (PITUITARY) GLAND
Heavy dots locate gland which makes the growing hormone (pituitrin).

own special gland and carries its own special order. Right now you are growing taller because of the growing hormone.

You grow in many ways as you grow up. You grow taller of course, but there are other changes, too, very important ones. These are the changes from boy to man or from girl to woman. Some of these changes you can see, like the beginning of a beard on a boy's face or the rounding out of a girl's figure. But the most important changes are going on inside, getting your body ready to be a father or mother some day. What tells your body to start making these changes?

The answer is hormones. At the right time, special glands make special growing-up hormones that direct and control the complicated growing-up process. These hormones are released a little at a time into the blood, which carries the growing-up message all over the body. The whole story of growing up is a book in itself. There are books about it and you may want to read one.*

The Speed Hormone

There's another important hormone—one whose job seems rather simple at first. A gland or clump of cells in your neck sends this hormone into your blood, telling each cell how fast to burn its food. That is, a little more of this speed hormone causes the food to be burned rapidly; a little less means slower burning.

Well, since everybody burns food, what difference does it make if the burning is just a little bit slower or faster?

Let's remember that food is burned *everywhere* in your body—not only in your muscle cells, but also in the cells of your skin, bone, nerves, in all the hundreds

---

* Try *The Wonder of Life* by Levine and Seligmann or *Growing Up* by De Schweinitz.

of different kinds of cells of which you're made. When the burning is a bit faster or slower, all the different kinds of cells do their work a bit faster or slower. All the tiny differences added together help to make *your* way of doing things just a bit different from anybody else's. And just a very slight amount of the speed hormone makes the difference.

That tiny bit more or tiny bit less is one of the reasons why you can find so many different types of

SPEED (THYROID) GLAND

Heavy dots locate gland which makes the speed hormone (thyroxin).

139

people in your neighborhood. There are the ones who are always saying "Come on! Let's get going" and the ones who say "Relax. What's the hurry?" and the many in between.

Of course, every healthy, happy person is interested in all kinds of things. The difference is that the extra-active people, the ones who have a bit more of the speed hormone, seem to prefer hurry-up things done in a hurry-up way. Those who burn their food more slowly seem to go in for a calmer, more quiet way of enjoying themselves. But all of us can do all the things—fast, slow or medium.

The Emergency Hormone

You can't feel the speed hormone at work on your cells. But there is another hormone whose work you *can* feel. You feel it when you walk into your dark bedroom at night and see what looks like a strange person lying on the bed. Remember how your heart begins to pound and how queer your stomach feels? Of course, when you finally snap on the light, the strange person turns out to be nothing more than the coat and hat that you had forgotten to put away. But, in the meantime, another hormone has started a lot of things working. This hormone prepares you for fight or flight, or any emergency action.

This hormone is made in two glands at the top of your kidneys. Usually the hormone is kept in its place, quiet as a fire-alarm box. But when the brain sends a message that something dangerous or exciting is about to happen, the emergency hormone is squirted into your blood. Then, as the blood swirls through your body,

EMERGENCY (ADRENAL) GLANDS
Heavy dots locate glands which make the emergency hormone (adrenaline).

the signals flash to your body cells and a whole series of amazing things happen:

1. Your liver sends out lots of stored-up food to be carried by the blood to your muscles. You remember that the muscles get their power through the burning of food. A special supply of food is needed for the special emergency you may have to handle. Jumping out of the way of a truck, chasing a runaway puppy, making a mad dash across the room to catch your little sister who has followed the cat to the top of the bookshelves —things like that need quick energy.

2. The air passages in your nose, windpipe, and lungs open up wide to permit more air to come in with each breath. You need more air to burn the food faster, to give you the energy for a quick, hard spurt or a long pull.

3. Your heart beats more powerfully, so that the blood with the food and air in it is sent swirling more quickly to your muscle cells.

4. The blood tubes that bring blood to your stomach and intestine close down. The digestion of food is put off for a while, because you need as much blood as possible in the muscles that will do the fighting or running, and in the brain that will do the thinking.

You can almost feel the blood leaving your middle when you get into a quarrel.

5. Something happens to your blood to protect you. If you should cut yourself during the emergency, the blood will clot more quickly, so that bleeding will stop sooner than it usually does.

6. The blood supply in your skin is cut down, making your skin become pale. The extra blood is sent to the muscles.

And still other things happen. All together the action of the emergency hormone adds up to this—that your body and brain are ready to handle emergencies almost as soon as you know about them.

There are many, many hormones in your body, each doing its own special job of message-carrying. Some of them work all the time while others go into action only at special times. All of them play an important part in the way you grow up and in making you the kind of person you are.

10. You Can Help Your Body Work

It's amazing, the things your body can do. Every second of the day and night, year in and year out, your body adjusts itself to work at its best for you. As you read quietly your heart beats slowly, because your muscle cells need little food and oxygen when you sit still. When you take time out for a romp with your dog, your heart automatically beats faster.

When you eat a doughnut your body digests some of the doughnut material into fat, and stores the fat under your skin. Some other time, when you go rowing and have to fight a stiff wind on the way home, that same fat will be changed into food for your muscles. When you are out in the hot sun, your skin cells form a brownish material that allows some of the sunlight, but not too much, to enter your cells. In hundreds of different ways your body adjusts itself to do the best possible job for you. It even protects you against invasion.

In the air that you breathe, in the food that you eat, on the ground that you walk, are billions of tiny cells called GERMS. There are many kinds of germs. Most

144

kinds are harmless, but a few kinds, like diphtheria or typhoid germs, are harmful. If the harmful kinds can get into your body, they can make you sick. But most of the time they don't stand a chance because your body has many ways of keeping germs out and of destroying them if they do get in.

If germs come in with the air that you breathe, they get caught in the sticky lining of your nose and windpipe. If germs come in with the food that you eat, the juices of your digestive system can usually take care of them, or they go right through the intestine and are gotten rid of together with the waste.

Sometimes germs can get inside your body through a break in the skin, like when you get a splinter or cut yourself. That's when your special police—the white cells in your blood—get to work.

The white cells ride all around your body like police patrol cars on the highway. You have thousands of white cells in every drop of blood. Ordinarily they just ride around, but when there is an invasion of germs, the white cells get busy. As blood flows near the germs, these white police cells work their way right out of the blood tubes to the germs that may cause trouble. The white cells don't waste any time. They surround the germs to keep them from spreading—and then they destroy them. The white cells pour juices on the germs which usually make them harmless in a short while.

The blood, together with the billions of red cells that carry oxygen, and the liquid that carries food and other materials, and the collected wastes, and the white cells, goes on its way with not a second's delay in the service. No machine, no locomotive, no car, no furnace has ever been invented that can defend itself from an invasion of harmful attackers.

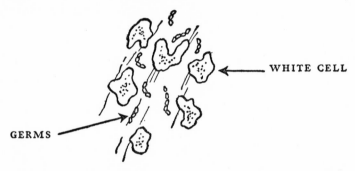

GERMS AND WHITE CELLS GREATLY ENLARGED

The white cells and the germs are too small for us to see without a powerful microscope. Otherwise you'd find it very interesting to watch the battle between the attackers (germs) and the defenders (white cells). But you do get a view of the battlefield when you look at a pus pimple. A pimple is a place where white cells are busy surrounding and attacking some germs. The yellowish pus consists of millions of white cells together with millions of germs. Some of them are dead and others are being finished off by the white cells.

The white cells can't always handle the job by themselves. Sometimes the attacking germs of some disease, like diphtheria, are too many or too powerful for the defending white cells, and then you become sick. The doctor says you have an infection, and he treats you with medicine whose job it is to help kill off the attacking germs, or to make harmless the poisons that the germs give off. Sometimes the doctor can do better than that. He can give you injections or "shots" of various kinds, that prepare your body ahead of time to fight certain dangerous disease germs. Then, if these germs come in, you don't get sick. Most of the time, however, your own white cells take care of things pretty well.

But your body is not a magician. It can't pull rabbits out of an empty hat. It can only give you good service if you give it good care. And it's easy to give your body the good care it deserves. Now that you know something about what goes on inside, the few simple needs of a healthy body are easy to understand. These few simple needs have to do mostly with food and rest.

Good Teeth For Good Eating

Lions and tigers don't usually have trouble with their teeth. But neither do they go to the movies or learn how to spell Mississippi. Nor do they eat angel cake, noodles, and other good foods that leave a mushy deposit in the spaces between the teeth. Germs enjoy the moist soft mush. When they get in, the mush rots and forms a substance that can slowly dissolve the hard enamel of your teeth. This makes a hole or cavity. Inside the cavity there are blood vessels, nerves, and a toothache. Brushing your teeth properly helps to scrub out the material that makes cavities.

The Right Food For The Job

Chocolate is good to eat and is a good body fuel. It might be pleasant to live on nothing but chocolate bars —no table to set, no dishes to wash. But if we did, it would be like a man who uses gasoline for every part of his car. He puts it in the tank to make the motor run, and that works out fine. But when he tries to fix a flat tire by dipping it in gasoline, and when he tries to repair the motor by pouring gasoline over it, the results are not so good.

In a car, gasoline is a good fuel for making the motor run, but gasoline is not good for repairing or replacing worn-out parts of the car. In your body, certain foods like chocolate bars are good fuels for burning in your muscle cells. But they can't be used to repair cells or make new ones. We need to leave room and appetite for other foods that do these important jobs.

Of course, there's nothing wrong with concentrating on sweets once in a while. Imagine a birthday cake made of whole wheat bread, iced with mashed potatoes, trimmed with peas and carrots and birthday candles.

Aside from birthday parties and other such occasions, we need to get a variety of foods. The right amount of each kind is called a BALANCED DIET. We need foods that burn well, for fuel. Potatoes, bread and butter, and cereals are fine for that job. We need other foods for growing and for repair. Milk, meat, fish, eggs, fruits and vegetables are good for these jobs.

This picture shows how to choose a balanced diet.

Choosing the right foods would be so simple if your body could just send a message saying "Pass the milk, please. I need it for building teeth." But the only message your body can send is "I'm hungry." It can't tell you which part of your body needs what food, but every part needs to be fed.

Raw Salads
Cole Slaw
Raw Carrots
Sliced Tomatoes

Custard~
Ice Cream
Cheese & Jelly
Milk Puddings

Milk ~
Cocoa~
Malted Milk
Buttermilk

Muffins
Cakes
Breads
Pies~
Pastry

However, eating the right food is only part of the story. The rest of the story is just as important, and has to do with *how* you eat the food.

Mealtime should be relaxed. Your digestive system works better when your mind and body are relaxed. The digestive juices flow freely and your food gets a good send-off on its way to becoming part of you. But when you use dinner as the time for settling accounts with your kid brother, or when you insist on having your favorite gangster program blaring away right through mealtime, you become tense. Then other things happen, one of which is that the emergency hormone is released into your blood.

That's the hormone that strengthens your breathing and heartbeat, increases the blood supply to your muscles, and *cuts down on the blood supply to your digestive system*. With less blood supply, digestion is slowed up and disturbed.

For most of us, then, the matter of food comes down to some simple, common-sense ideas:

1. Good teeth, properly cared for, to chew the food.

2. A balanced diet—enough food—the right kind to take care of your body's needs.

3. Pleasant, relaxed mealtimes, with a short time of relaxation afterward to give your meal a good start on its way to becoming part of you.

Grow While You Sleep

Sometimes it seems as if all the most interesting things happen after your bedtime, while the grown-ups are still up. But you need more sleep than grown-ups do because, believe it or not, your body works harder.

A grown-up's body has two jobs to do, but your body has three.

1. Everybody, whether he is one day or a hundred years old, *needs to clear out waste material* formed by the burning in the cells.

2. Everybody, any age, needs to *replace worn-out cells.*

3. Your growing body has a third job, *to grow and make more cells* than you are wearing out. The best time for this job is when you're at rest or asleep. That's why you need more sleep than a person who is finished growing.

How much sleep is enough? People vary, but up to ten years old, you probably need eleven or twelve hours. At eleven you need about eleven hours. Up to thirteen years, about ten or eleven hours should do. If you've had that much good sleep in a quiet, airy room and still don't feel fresh in the morning, you may even need more sleep for a while until your body catches up with its work.

Easy On The Eyes

Look at the gentleman in the picture. As you might guess, his legs and back will soon be tired. But so will his eyes. Although most people don't read in this peculiar position, they do other things that are just as bad for the eyes. They read in all sorts of queer positions, in dim light, in moving cars and busses. But what's harmful about all that?

Reading in queer positions is hard work for the muscles that move your eyeballs as you follow the words. They have been trained to do their work with your head in an upright position. In other positions they have to learn their job over again, and that's extra work. You can get an idea of what this is like by trying to write sideways like this:

You're using the same muscles as when you write in the usual way, but it's harder work because your muscles are not used to this queer way of working.

Reading in a dim light is also a strain on muscles—the iris or window-shade muscles. They regulate the amount of light that comes through into the back of your eyes. In a dim light, some of the muscles have to pull hard in order to make a large opening for the light to come through, and pretty soon they become tired. You can feel what it's like by "making a muscle" in your arm and keeping it that way. Even though you're not lifting anything with your muscle, it will soon feel tired from the tightened position.

Reading in a moving car or bus is hard on lots of muscles. The bumping and shaking makes extra work for your eyeball muscles as they try to follow the jiggling book. At the same time the changing light—a flash of sunlight, a shady spot, another flash of sunlight—causes your iris muscles to work overtime trying to regulate the light. And still at the same time, your lens muscles are working furiously, changing the shape of the lens in each eye. Every time the book jiggles toward or away from you, the lens shape must be changed in order for you to see the words clearly. So you see that this kind of reading means quite a struggle for lots of muscles.

You'll find that reading is much easier on your eyes if you sit up comfortably, with the light coming over your shoulder from behind you. When you write, if you're right-handed, have the light come from over your left shoulder, so that your pen or pencil doesn't cast a shadow over your writing. When you read one of those shiny, slick-paper magazines, hold the magazine in a position where you can see the printing clearly without a glare of reflected light from the shiny paper.

Falling Apart?

In the comic books, on the radio, in the magazines and newspapers, in the bus and train ads, there are terrible warnings of the hopeless and shameful things that will happen to you unless you buy this, drink that, smell the other, smear something else. If you believed them all, you'd have to spend twenty-four hours a day to keep from falling apart.

The people who write those ads are paid to think up things that will make you rush out to the store to buy their product. One way of getting you there is to scare you by telling you of all the sicknesses that will attack you unless you use Jonesberry's Snake Oil Balm for A Movie Star Complexion. Another way is to shame you by telling you about the whispering going on behind your back because you don't wash with Steeple's Soap, the Soap that Makes you Smell Higher than a Spire.

Don't let any ad shame you or scare you. When you don't feel well, see a doctor. Don't let an advertising writer be your family doctor. He wasn't trained for it.

Just keep in mind that your body is more wonderful than all the machines ever invented, and that if it gets reasonably good care in the matter of food and rest, it can usually take care of itself for many long, happy years.

Index